The Gift of Holy Spirit

Every Christian's Divine Deposit

By

Mark H. Graeser

John A. Lynn

John W. Schoenheit

Note: Most Scriptures quoted in this book are from *The New International Version* (*NIV*). References taken from other translations or versions will be noted, i.e., *King James Version* = (*KJV*). In verses quoted, words in all capital letters indicate our own emphasis.

(*NIV*) = *New International Version*

Scripture taken from *THE HOLY BIBLE, NEW INTERNATIONAL VERSION*. Copyright © 1973, 1978, 1984 International Bible Society. Used by permission of Zondervan Publishing House.

Scripture quotations marked (Amplified) are taken from *The Amplified Bible,* Old Testament, copyright © 1995, 1987 by Zondervan Corporation. *The Amplified New Testament,* copyright © 1954, 1958, 1987 by the Lockman Foundation. Used by permission.

Scripture quotations marked (*RSV*) are taken from *The Revised Standard Version,* copyright © 1952.

ISBN 0-9628971-3-2

FIRST EDITION

©1995

Published by

CHRISTIAN EDUCATIONAL SERVICES, INC.
(Referred to in footnotes as CES)

POST OFFICE BOX 30336

INDIANAPOLIS, INDIANA 46230

Table of Contents

Appendix B:

Appendix C:

Acknowledgments

First, and most importantly, we are thankful to our Heavenly Father and His wonderful Son Jesus Christ for their love for us, and for the assurance of faith they have given to every believer.

We are also thankful for all the men and women from whom we have learned through the years, and whose thoughts and ideas contributed to this work.

We are especially thankful to the following people who helped in preparing this work:

Editing: Jim Landmark, Pat Lynn, Ivan Maddox, Scott Pfeiffer and Greg Pharis.

Cover Design: Wayne Harms

Layout design: Joe Ramon

Topical Index and Scripture Index: Suzanne Snyder

Typing and Proofreading: Pat Lynn

Preface

Jesus Christ said that knowing the truth will make one free (John 8:32). We assert that the converse is equally true: believing erroneous teaching puts you in some degree of bondage, proportionate to the importance and practical relevance of the particular truth in question. Bondage means a restriction or restraint upon one's freedom to enjoy the blessings of God and a life of service to Him. The subject addressed in this book is *absolutely vital* for each and every Christian [1] to understand, both for his own personal spiritual fulfillment and for the harmonious functioning of the Body of Christ as a whole.

God's Adversary, the Devil, knows that if Christians stand together on the truth of God's Word, they will regularly defeat him. Therefore, he is always doing his best to destroy the unity of the Body of Christ by trying to get as many Christians as he can to believe things contrary to the Word of God, and thus divide them. In this book, we will expose some of the chief lies he is using today among Christians, and in contrast set forth the pertinent scriptural truths for your consideration. When it comes to any spiritual matter, the written Word of God is our only rule of faith and practice. Our purpose is not to be contentious, but to speak the truth in love for the benefit of our precious brethren in the Lord.

Satan is very adept at "using a Christian's own momentum," if you will, to get him "off the track." The issue to be covered in this book does not pertain to Christians who could be described as "lukewarm." They are in little danger of falling prey to the particular ploy in question. Rather, it is those who are avidly seeking to walk in all the power of God who are susceptible. Many such saints are found in what are today called "Pentecostal" or "Charismatic" groups. They are like those who Paul described as "zealous for God, but their zeal is not based upon knowledge" (Romans 10:2).

---

1. To define this key term at the outset, we assert that a "Christian" is a person who has done what Romans 10:9 says ("That if you confess with your mouth 'Jesus is Lord' and believe in your heart that God raised him from the dead, you will be saved.") and who thus has received from the Lord Jesus Christ the gift of holy spirit, the "divine nature" of God the Father, and thereby become a son of God.

In such circles, "spiritual experiences" and "sincerity" are too often given priority over the written Word of God as the criterion to determine doctrinal truth and the practical application of it. Too often, Christians use their experiences to validate the Word of God, rather than allowing the written Word to be the ultimate "discerner" (critic—Hebrews 4:12) of all "things that pertain to life and godliness" (II Peter 1:3). This leaves them open to counterfeit spiritual experiences.

Only an expert in the details of the genuine can easily recognize a clever counterfeit. We believe that too many Christians have been lulled into a complacent attitude toward the written Word of God. This is in vivid contrast to the example of our Lord and Savior Jesus Christ, who expressed His basis for life with the words, "It is written." When one learns, believes and obeys the Word of God, he will have genuine, godly experiences that will not only enhance his relationship with his heavenly Father, but also deepen his commitment to serve others the bread of life.

The conflict between the truths of Scripture, which may or may not have specific emotional appeal, and experiences, which are by nature exciting and impressive, has been going on for centuries. The appeal of God's Word is primarily rational, because God gives *evidence* for belief. When Christ sent out his disciples, they "returned with joy" because of what they had experienced. They said "Lord, even the demons submit to us" (Luke 10:12). Christ then reminded them, "Do not rejoice that the demons submit to you, but rejoice that your names are written in heaven" (Luke 10:20). The same tension exists today. Many Christians rejoice at experiences like miracles and healings, but do not rejoice at the powerful and basic truths of God's Word. This is putting the cart before the horse.

Certainly, genuine spiritual phenomena are to be expected in the life of a Christian, but too many Christians have been uncritical in their examination of such phenomena. The Bible gives many examples of false prophets who deceived people by demonstrations of spiritual power. The magicians of Egypt did turn sticks into snakes, but their power was not from the true God. God gives instructions in His Word as to what He will and will not do, so it is by examining one's experiences in light of the Word of God that the power or force behind the experience can be determined.

Speaking about the written Word of God, Jesus Christ said, "Thy Word is truth" (John 17:17). When it comes to spiritual things beyond the realm of man's five senses, the Word of God is the *only* credible witness. In stark contrast to the vague, groundless theories and speculations originating in the minds of men, God, the Author of life, presents clear, straightforward answers to the most profound questions of the human heart. Thus we must look into God's Word, the literature of eternity, and let Him speak for Himself about the deep issues of life.

The Bible is the standard of all literature, and God the Author of all authors. As literature, it contains a rich variety of linguistic thoughts, expressions and usages. Like any author, God has the right to use language as He deems appropriate to His purposes. E.W. Bullinger, an eminent British Bible scholar (1837-1913), identified the use of more than 200 figures of speech in the Bible. These figures greatly enrich its literary value and at the same time entrust its readers with great responsibility.

Those who endeavor to study, understand and interpret the Bible must become very sensitive to the literary devices it employs, because its study is not merely for cultural amusement. Our very lives, both temporal and eternal, depend on an accurate understanding of God's words, which are the very "words of life."

When God makes statements of fact or uses language in the way it is normally used, we should surely take note. When He departs from customary usage of words, syntax, grammar and statements true to fact, we must take double note, for such departures serve to better communicate truth than can literal statements of fact.

As the only credible witness of eternal and spiritual verities, the Bible gives testimony in a variety of ways—some literal, some figurative. Misconstruing the use of its language is one of the principal errors of the orthodox Christian Church, particularly, as we shall see, regarding the subject of holy spirit. This has resulted in the Word of God being twisted, distorted and misrepresented.

God chose to communicate the great truths of eternity via the medium of words. It is our firm conviction that when properly translated and understood, the Bible will integrally fit together without contradictions. Like the pieces of a jigsaw puzzle depicting a stunningly beautiful scene, every single verse in the Word of God will (and must) fit into the total picture. Many of the erroneous teachings in Christianity today survive only because the total scope of Scripture is not taken into account. Verses that do not fit into "traditional" theology are either ignored or explained away with less than honest and exacting biblical scholarship.

We do not consider ourselves the fount of all spiritual wisdom, and we do not present this book as the last word on the subject. We do believe, however, both from our study of God's Word and our own experience, that what is taught today in many Pentecostal and Charismatic groups has very harmful implications in the lives of Christians. We ask you to consider the biblical and logical validity of our thesis, and decide its merit for yourself.

Introduction

I t is our contention that a very subtle and divisive error has crept into the Church to the degree that it has left many believers who have embraced it either "puffed up" or deflated. Our purpose in this book is to identify and correct this error for the benefit of anyone already afflicted by it, and for those who may encounter it in the future. As with every spiritual matter, our unwavering standard to distinguish truth from error is the written Word of God.

Today, anyone familiar with what is happening in Christian circles constantly hears a number of related biblical terms misused to describe *some* Christians, but not *all* Christians. In logic, "all" means that *every* member of one set (or category) is also a member of another set. "None" means that no member of one set is a member of another set. "Some" is a set that includes the range from one less than all to one more than none. There is obviously a world of difference between "all" and "some," as in "ALL Scripture is God-breathed..." (II Timothy 3:16). If it said, "SOME Scripture...", how would we determine which is which?

If only "some" Christians are "anointed," "spirit-filled" and "baptized in the holy spirit," what determines why some receive this blessing and some don't? As you will see, the erroneous use of these terms has caused much confusion. Scripture warns us of such malady in the Church when it speaks of Christians being "tossed about by every wind of doctrine" (Ephesians 4:14).

As we will see, the Bible figuratively likens the gift of holy spirit to a liquid substance. This is evident in the following terms currently being misused by many believers:

(1) "Baptized in the Holy Spirit"

This phrase is used to teach that sometime after one's new birth, God gives the "Holy Spirit" to him. This "baptism in the Holy Spirit" enables him to walk with God in a new and more powerful way.

(2) "Anointed" or "the anointing"

These terms are used to describe a more advanced, equipped or spiritual state for a Christian. They are also used to describe a temporary spiritual enabling.

(3) "Spirit-filled" or "filled with the Holy Spirit"

These phrases are used to describe a more mature Christian who has received the "gifts" of the Holy Spirit, particularly speaking in tongues.

This terminology is used throughout Christendom today by many well-meaning believers. If you are among them, please understand that it is not our intent to offend you, but to set before you what we believe is the correct understanding of these terms as they are used in Scripture, in the hope that it will enhance your walk with the Lord. The central thesis of this study is that *all Christians have been given the same power of God, and each has avenues to utilize that power.*

Certainly this thesis should, on the surface, be more appealing than the idea that some Christians have less power than others. To argue for the latter is to argue for a lesser possibility, much like the argument that each Christian has only *some* of the nine "gifts" of the spirit, or that the "one baptism" of Ephesians 4:5 is water, rather than holy spirit. Arguing for a lesser possibility is far too common among Christians today. We have a BIG God, who wants to do BIG things in, with and for *each Christian* (Ephesians 3:20). Let us allow Him to speak for Himself in His Word about these matters.

Scripture teaches that the Body of Christ is like the human body, in that no part is unimportant or greater than another. Each is essential to the fluid working of the whole. So it is with the spiritual body—the Church. We may not all have the same function, but we can each function with the power that our Lord has given to us. The teaching that in the Church there are the "haves" and the "have nots" has engendered frustration, hurt, jealously and even hatred. The following quote is an example of such teachings:

> After you make Jesus the Lord of your life, it is the will of God that you experience the fullness of the Holy Spirit...So, to be born again and not to be filled with the Spirit is like being on a train without a track. [2]

Would God make you "a train" without giving you "a track" to run on? The premise that one can be born again yet not be filled with holy spirit demeans the greatness of the new birth. It sounds as though a Christian who is "only" born again is virtually "spiritless"

---

2. Kenneth Copeland, "Tongue Talking Tenacity" (*The Believer's Voice of Victory* Magazine, Ft. Worth TX, January, 1993, Vol. 21, No. 1), page 18.

and powerless. As we will see, God's Word states that every person who gets born again is, at that moment, filled with holy spirit. If we could correct the above statement, we would say, "So, to be born again and not KNOW YOU ARE filled with the spirit is like being on a train without a track." Later, we will explain the fullness of all that God gives each person at the moment of his new birth.

Let us now examine another too-typical teaching concerning the terms we previously listed.

> I believe there at least three types of Spirit baptism. The first is what I call the baptism *of* the Holy Spirit. I think it occurs at the point of conversion...The second type of Holy Spirit baptism is what I call the baptism *in* the Holy Spirit...To be baptized *in* the Spirit is to filled with the Spirit. Although this baptism in the Spirit can occur at conversion, it usually happens at a later time. It is a result of learning how to walk with the Lord in obedience to His will...The third type of Spirit baptism is what I call the baptism *by* the Holy Spirit. It is the special anointing that God gives a person to empower him for service in the kingdom. [3]

We believe this quote is indicative of the current confusion among many sincere saints resulting from a lack of clear definition of biblical terms. In contrast to the above writer's "three baptisms," Ephesians 4:5 states that there is *one baptism*. Here again we must emphasize that the written Word of God takes precedence over sincere Christian opinion. What is at stake is not only the integrity of God's Word, but also our practical application of it to the end of true Christian unity.

We will now note one more example of the current misunderstandings in regard to this issue, in which the writer suggests that a *Christian* pray the following prayer to receive "the Holy Spirit."

> Heavenly Father, I thank You for the promise of Your Spirit. Jesus, You are my Savior. I trust You now by grace through faith. You are the One who baptizes with the Holy Spirit. I'm not waiting for any sign or feeling to believe that You

---

3. David R. Reagan, "Holy Spirit Baptism", *Bible Prophecy Insights*, No. 61 (Lamb & Lion Ministries, McKinney TX, November 1992) page 2.

have baptized me with the Holy Spirit. I receive your gift. Thank You that I am now a Spirit-filled child of God. Amen. [4]

It certainly appears that the writer believes that the "promise of the Spirit," the "baptism of the Holy Spirit," and being "Spirit-filled" are not included in the new birth. Please understand that we are in no way trying to demean or belittle the work of such Christians. We know that they are sincere and do love God. We thank God for them and the deliverance their ministries produce. It is just that we see the potential for more power and more unity among Christians if we all were more attentive to the vocabulary of Scripture.

In this study, we will see that the Word of God makes it clear that the way God becomes our Father is by birthing us, and in that birth we receive the fullness of His divine nature, which is referred to as holy spirit. Also, as we will see, there *is* a sign by which each Christian can know that at the moment of his new birth he received God's gift and was filled with His spirit.

Does the Bible really teach that there is more spiritual power or ability a Christian can receive from the Lord than that which he received at the moment of his new birth? If not, how appalling it is that Christians are being taught to ask and wait for something they already have. It reminds us of the account of the man who died thinking he was penniless, when in reality he had inherited a fortune of which he had no knowledge. How many wonderful Christians have done their best to love God and walk according to His Word, yet remained frustrated because they felt they were never good enough to receive the "special anointing" they thought they needed from God?

As in the days of old, God's people are still being hindered and destroyed because of lack of knowledge (Hosea 4:6). That is why we will examine what God's Word says about each of the terms we set forth earlier. If you have been confused and frustrated because of the misuse of these terms, it will bless you immensely to learn that when you confessed Jesus as Lord and believed that God raised Him from the dead (Romans 10:9), you received a magnificent gift from

---

4. "Empowered By The Spirit," by Harald Bredesen, *Charisma* Magazine, August 1994) page 49.

the Lord Jesus— the gift of holy spirit, containing all you will ever need to manifest the love and power of God. At that moment, you were once and for all *born again, anointed, baptized with the holy spirit* and forever *filled* (to capacity) *with holy spirit*— the divine nature of God.

This is every Christian's divine deposit. One of the dictionary definitions of the word "deposit" is "anything given as security or in partial payment." We will see that God's divine deposit He has already given to each Christian is only a token of what He will one day do for us. The word "deposit" is also defined as "anything laid away or entrusted to another for safekeeping." God has placed this gift in us and entrusted us to use it to His glory. However, if we do not know what we have, the precious gift will lie dormant within us, locked away in the vault of our hearts.

Why do we call this divine deposit "a liquid asset"? Because we want to echo God's terminology, and it was He who chose such liquid-related terms as "anointed," "baptized," "filled," and "poured out." Then we looked up the word "liquid" in the dictionary, and we struck oil—liquid gold! Listen to this:

> That which is extremely fluid...so as to flow freely...and to have a definite volume without having a definite shape, except such as is temporarily given by a container...[Regarding assets], capable of being readily converted into cash. [5]

Isn't this a wonderful metaphor of what the spiritual "deposit" in a Christian is to be? We have each been given a definite "volume" of holy spirit—we are *filled!* Each of our earthen vessels temporarily determines its shape, that is, what the spirit "looks like" as it flows freely in our individual lives. Like the fountain of living waters from whence our holy spirit came, we can bubble up from within, no matter what our circumstances, and be as fluid as necessary to do the will of God. Our internal asset is definitely convertible to "cash," that is, the resources we need to give away to others. What's more, we can do so without diminishing our account balance!

In examining God's divine deposit, we will see why being "born again" is a must for every human being who desires true *life.*

---

5. *Webster's Third New International Dictionary* (R.R. Donnelley and Sons, The Lakeside Press, Chicago IL, 1966), page 1319.

Then we will look at what it means to be born again, and what one receives in his new birth. We will examine the vital difference between the Giver (God, the Holy Spirit) and the gift of His divine nature (holy spirit). Next we will consider the subject of water in Scripture, and then set forth what God's Word says about each of the pertinent "liquid" terms being used so haphazardly today.

After that, we will see that the *one gift* of holy spirit has a number of *manifestations* that are readily available to every Christian. In closing, we will set forth from Scripture your completeness in Christ, and upon that basis exhort you to walk boldly in Him. Too many Christians today are, in effect, unknowingly sitting on a toolbox full of precision tools and praying for God to build them something. Too many are, as it were, sitting in their powerful new cars hoping God will start them. What we are setting forth in this book will help you *turn the key and take off!*

Our goal is to clarify these very practical truths from the pages of God's Word, so that you can see who you are as a son of God, what you have in Christ and what you can do for others. We hope that enough believers will benefit from this understanding so as to eliminate much of the unnecessary confusion, division and frustration that the misuse of these terms has caused. We pray that your heart will burn within you as the simplicity of God's Word (His heart to us) is set before you, that you will rejoice in all you have been freely given and that you will walk your personal path of righteousness with peace, joy and the power of love.

Chapter 1

God's Divine Deposit In You

Why Be "Born Again?"

T he above question must be briefly answered before we go
on to see what is received in the package of life that the
Lord gives each person who believes in Him. The reason
each person since the day of Pentecost [6] must be born
again in order to have life in the age to come [7] is because the first time
we were born (physically), we each inherited the sin nature of our
"father" Adam, and thus were born *dead* in sin (Ephesians 2:1, etc.).
Because of this "death" nature in us, our physical lives are doomed
to end in death. The following verses show us both the problem and
its solution.

I Corinthians 15:21,22

For since death came through a man, the resurrection of the
dead comes also through a man.

For as in Adam all die, so in Christ all will be made alive.

How did death come to us from Adam? The Bible tells us
(Genesis 2:7) that God made Adam's body from the dust of the
ground, and then breathed into that body the breath of life, making
him a living soul, or being. He put Adam on a perfect earth and gave
him some basic instructions.

Genesis 2:16,17

And the Lord God commanded the man, "You are free to eat
from any tree in the garden; but you must not eat from the
tree of the knowledge of good and evil, for when you eat of
it you will surely die."

Romans 6:23 tells us that the wages of sin is death. When
Adam sinned, he sentenced himself to the punishment of death God
had warned him about. He sentenced not only himself to death, but

---

6. Later on we will develop the time distinction regarding Pentecost.

---

7. We use the phrase "the age to come" instead of the commonly-used phrase
"eternal life" *(aionion zoe),* because the actual promise of *aionion zoe* (literally "age
life") refers to "life in the coming age," the future Paradise that the prophets spoke
of. The contemporary translation of *aionion zoe,* "eternal life," was not in the mind
of the writers of Holy Scripture. See *Is There Death After Life?* (Fourth Edition),
pages 32 and 33, and the CES tape "The Kingdom of God, Paradise Regained."

the whole human race, which, as his offspring, were born dead in sin. In Adam's case, due to his originally perfect genetic make-up and the perfection of his environment, which then slowly began to disintegrate, he lived 930 years. Adam passed on to all his offspring the heritage of sin and death, as the history of man so grievously attests, and as the following verse shows:

Romans 5:12

Therefore, just as sin entered the world through one man, and death through sin, and in this way death came to all men, because all sinned.

Because each human being has inherited the sin nature of Adam, each will inevitably sin, and each is required to pay the penalty for sin, which is death. In His grace and mercy, God has provided mankind with a substitute, His Son Jesus Christ, who died in our place to pay the required penalty. By being obedient unto death, Jesus Christ made it possible for God to raise Him from the dead. Thus Jesus, "the last Adam" (I Corinthians 15:45), conquered death and can now give everlasting life to those who by faith in Him appropriate unto themselves what He made available.

The gift of holy spirit that Christ gives to each person who believes on Him as Lord is not in itself everlasting life, but rather the guarantee of life in the age to come (Ephesians 1:13,14). Thus, each Christian is from the moment of his new birth a three-fold person of body, soul and holy spirit. If a Christian is taught that he does not have holy spirit, it is tantamount, in practice, to consigning him to live in spiritual incompleteness, like the First Adam after the fall.

Biblically speaking, to be "born again" (I Peter 1:23; I John 3:9; 4:7; 5:1 et al) is synonymous with being "saved." [8] The word "saved" comes from the Greek word *sozo,* which means "to make whole; to rescue; to deliver." A Christian's ultimate salvation is his being

---

8. We are showing in this book that when a person is "saved," it is synonymous with being "born again," and that it is at the time of his new birth that he receives holy spirit (which is "born" in him). The Christian is a child of God (I John 3:1; Galatians 4:5-7), has a new nature (II Corinthians 5:17), is righteous (II Corinthians 5:21), is justified (Romans 5:1), is sanctified (I Corinthians 1:2), is a holy one (Romans 1:7; I Corinthians 1:2, etc., often translated as "saint"), has been redeemed (Galatians 3:13), is reconciled to God (Colossians 1:22), and is at peace with God (Romans 5:1). Thus the Word of God is clear concerning the finished work of the Lord Jesus Christ in a Christian.

saved from everlasting death, but "salvation" also includes spiritual wholeness now so that we can walk with God in this life.

Each and every Christian receives the gift of holy spirit at the moment of his new birth. It is not something he gets later. It is not something he somehow "earns," "prays for," or that is given when he is "spiritually qualified." Remember, holy spirit is a *gift*, not a reward, given to help transform us into the image of Christ. It comes when one is born of God. Thus we each have the potential to communicate intimately with our heavenly Father and to manifest to the world the very heart of Jesus Christ. The key is knowing what we have and how to use it.

What Is The New Birth?

Throughout Scripture, there are many analogies between things in the natural realm and corresponding things in the spiritual realm. God uses these to help us human beings, who do understand

---

Since all this is true of the Christian, why are there verses that seem to indicate that a Christian's salvation is not yet accomplished? The answer to that very good question lies in the way in which the words "saved" and "salvation" are used in the Word of God. Scripture contains quite a few words that have more than one meaning. The basic meaning of the word "save" is "to rescue." However, "save" and "salvation" are used in ways other than to mean salvation unto everlasting life. Some other New Testament usages include: saved from evil circumstances (Acts 7:25; Philippians 1:19), saved from starvation (Acts 17:34—translated "health" in *KJV*, "survive" in *NIV*, "preservation" in NASB), and saved from disease (Acts 4:9—translated "made whole" in *KJV*, "healed" in *NIV*, "made well" in *NASB*).

Often, "saved" does refer to salvation from everlasting death unto everlasting life. In such cases, the verb tense and the context make it clear that salvation is a completed work. There are, however, other verses that seem to say that our salvation is not complete or assured. In them, the word "salvation" is used of *behavioral* deliverance or wholeness. Although the work of Christ is spiritually complete and entire, the work of salvation in the physical realm, i.e. rescue and wholeness, is not yet complete. Christians still sin, get sick and in general suffer the consequences that living in this sinful world brings. Thus, when the Bible says that Christians "are being saved" (I Corinthians 1;18; II Corinthians 2:15) or to "work out your salvation "(Philippians 2;12), it is not referring to salvation from sin, but to the rescue and wholeness that relates to physical life. Each Christian is involved in a constant struggle to experience outwardly in his flesh the rescue and wholeness that Christ wrought for us spiritually. As the Christian walks forward with the Lord, he is in a very real sense "being saved."

the natural realm, understand spiritual truth also.   One such example is the idea of being "born again."

Think about a normal human birth— you know, "Wa-a-a-h!" There you were, a screaming bundle of life.   Why were you screaming? Because you were peeved about having to wait until later in life to get a *liver*?   No.   You "came from the factory" completely, completely complete, with *everything* you needed for growth perfectly packaged within you.

Why then would your *spiritual birth* leave you lacking something necessary for you to grow to spiritual maturity, something you must acquire later on in your spiritual life? It doesn't. We will see from Scripture that at the moment you are born again, that is, born of God, you received from your heavenly Father the gift of holy spirit—all you will ever need, the fullness of God in Christ in you, God's divine nature.

The first time you were born was because of a *seed*—one that your father gave your mother. Because of Adam's sin and death, it was a "corruptible" seed, that is, the life it generated will not last forever—it will eventually die. But when one is born again, he is born of incorruptible seed.

I Peter 1:23

For you have been born again, not of perishable seed, but of imperishable, through the living and enduring word of God. [9]

The imperishable seed is the very life of God planted within you in the gift of holy spirit. As a Christian, you are now endued with a new, divine nature, and you have the potential to be like your Father.

II Peter 1:2-4 (*KJV*)

Grace and peace be multiplied unto you through the knowledge of God, and of Jesus our Lord,

---

9. This verse is a wonderful example of the figure of speech *Ellipsis*, which is when a word that would ordinarily be in the text is left out to emphasize another word. In this verse, "imperishable" is an adjective and needs a noun to modify. We would expect the verse to read "born again, not of perishable seed, but of imperishable seed." By leaving out the second "seed," God emphasizes the *imperishability* of the seed. For more on *Ellipsis*, see E.W. Bullinger's *Figures Of Speech Used in the Bible*.

According as His divine power hath given unto us all things that pertain unto life and godliness, through the knowledge of Him that hath called us to glory and virtue;

Whereby are given unto us exceeding great and precious promises; that by these ye might be PARTAKERS OF THE DIVINE NATURE, having escaped the corruption that is in the world through lust.

In I Peter 1:23, we see that one's new, spiritual birth comes via hearing and believing the Word of God. II Peter 1:2 and 3 speak of the "knowledge of God and of Jesus our Lord" as the means by which we learn how to become partakers of the divine nature. It is in God's Word that one finds the knowledge of how to get born again. Where is this in the Word?

Romans 10:8-10

But what does it say? "The word is near you; it is in your mouth and in your heart, that is, the word of faith we are proclaiming:

That if you confess with your mouth, "Jesus is Lord," and believe in your heart that God raised him from the dead, you will be saved.

For it is with your heart that you believe and are justified, and it is with your mouth that you confess and are saved.

The "word of faith" is that Word of God one must believe in his heart if he wants to be saved. Saved from *what*? Death. What saves you from death? Life. How do you get life? Birth. Thus we see that to be "saved" is the same as to be born again. Simple, huh? Let's allow another section of Scripture to clarify just what it means to be "saved." Note the "liquid" terminology.

Titus 3:5,6 (*Amplified Bible*)

He saved us, not because of any works of righteousness that we had done, but because of His own pity *and* mercy, by [the] CLEANSING (BATH) of the new birth (regeneration) and renewing of the holy spirit [no article "the," read "of holy spirit"]. [10]

---

10. In this first, and in all subsequent biblical quotations in this book where we find the words "the holy spirit," we will note in brackets the proper rendering of the Greek text. Doing this will allow you to see for yourself how the translators of

Which He POURED OUT [so] richly upon us through Jesus Christ our Savior.

In these verses, we can clearly see that to be "saved" (from death) is to be born again and simultaneously receive new life in the gift of holy spirit. In the words "cleansing bath" and "poured out," we see the liquid analogy—the reason why we call God's divine deposit within us a "liquid asset." The word "richly" indicates that God did not hold back anything when He gave us the gift of holy spirit.

Three great statements of the Lord Jesus Christ's goodness follow the formula for salvation in Romans 10:9,10.

Romans 10:11-13

As the Scripture says, "Anyone who trusts in him will never be put to shame.

For there is no difference between Jew and Gentile— the same Lord is Lord of all and richly blesses all who call on him, for, Everyone who calls on the name of the Lord will be saved."

If you needed financial help, would you ask a poor man or a rich man? A poor man might desire to help you, but he would lack the means. A rich man has the means to help, if he wills to do so. The Lord Jesus became poor by giving His life for us, and God raised Him from the dead to the riches of a limitless inheritance (Hebrews 1:4). That is why He is rich unto *all* who call on Him. He gives a gift to each one. This gift is the holy spirit that Jesus received from God, and gives to each person who believes in Him as Lord. As we will see, *the first time* that the exalted Lord Jesus did this was on the Day of Pentecost (Acts 2:33). This gift of holy spirit is the "earnest" (Ephesians 1:14—*KJV*), or guarantee, that your "earthen vessel" will, at His appearing, be replaced by a perfect body like the Lord's.

---

different Bible versions have been influenced by theological bias and thus not held true to the text. Primarily, we will show where we believe the words "holy" and "spirit" should not be capitalized, and point out where the text has no article "the" preceding them. An explanation of the difference between "Holy Spirit" and "holy spirit," as well as when the article "the" is used, is given in the next section of this chapter. It is also often the case that translators use the masculine pronoun "him" when the Greek clearly reads the neuter pronoun "it," because their theology dictates that holy spirit is a "person" instead of a gift. We will point out those also.

The Giver And The Gift

I Corinthians 8:6 states that there is one God, the Father, and one Lord, Jesus Christ, and that every blessing a Christian receives originates with God and comes to him through Jesus Christ. God is the Giver of all life (Hebrews 2:10). It is He Who gave Jesus life in the womb of Mary (Luke 1:31-35), and it is He Who gave Him new life by raising Him from the dead and exalting Him as "Lord" (Philippians 2:8-11).

The One God, the Father, is holy, He is spirit and He is the "only True God" (John 17:3). Thus He often refers to Himself in His Word as "*the* Holy Spirit." [11] In English, we capitalize proper nouns, but most nouns mean the same thing whether or not they are capitalized. [12] When we speak of the "Holy Spirit" and the "holy spirit,"

---

11. In the Old Testament, God was occasionally known as "the Holy," which usually gets translated as "the Holy One." For example, II Kings 19:22 (*KJV*) says, "Whom hast thou reproached and blasphemed? And against whom hast thou exalted thy voice, and lifted up thine eyes on high? Even against the Holy *One* of Israel." Note that God is called "the Holy *One*" and that the word "one" is in italics, which is how the King James translators let the reader know the word was not in the Hebrew text (although it is implied). Most of the time, the King James translators did not put the word "one" in italics, even though it is *not* in the Hebrew text. This is a good example of the inconsistency that translators have shown in this field of the holy spirit. Some other references in the Old Testament where God is called "the Holy" are Job 6:10; Psalms 71:22; 78:41; 89:18 and Isaiah 1:4. Also, God is called "the Holy of Jacob" in Isaiah 29:33, and "your Holy" in Isaiah 43:15.

In the New Testament, God is still known as holy, as verses like Luke 1:49 and John 17:11 show. Thus it is easy to see why God, who is holy and who is spirit, would refer to Himself in the New Testament as "the Holy Spirit." This is especially true in the light of the New Testament teaching of Christ, because Christ is also known in the New Testament as the "Holy One" (Compare Mark 1:24; Luke 4:34; Acts 3:14 and I John 2:20). Furthermore, all those who believe in Christ are also called "holy ones," which has been translated as "saints" in most versions of the Bible.

The adjective "Holy" (usually translated "the Holy One," as we said) was not the only adjective used in place of God's name. For example, God is called "the Righteous [One]" in Isaiah 24:16, and in Mark 14:61 He is called "the Blessed [One]."

---

12. Some English nouns do have a different meaning when they are capitalized. Take, for example, the first names of the authors of this book. As only a "mark" on the wall of the "john," Mark would not have been able to help John and John write the book.

however, we are talking about very different things in the Bible. The "Holy Spirit" is God, the Father, the Giver, while the "holy spirit" is the gift of His divine nature that He gives to us by way of the Lord Jesus Christ. This is an absolutely *vital* truth that too few people have recognized.

There is much confusion among Christians about exactly what "God" does and exactly what "the Holy Spirit" does, because different verses seem to have them doing the same things. Most Bible readers are not taught that the word "spirit" has a considerable number of different usages, and so they are not sensitive to the context of each use. Further, the translators of the Bible have been very unhelpful because they have added to and/or subtracted from their translations of the Hebrew and Greek texts on hundreds of occasions, while not informing the reader that they have done so. Also, translators have used capital letters and lowercase letters based upon their own theology. The reader of the Bible needs to be aware that most ancient texts were either all capital letters or all lowercase letters. All capitalized distinctions, therefore, between "Spirit" and "spirit" are added. We realize that such distinctions can be contextually appropriate, but it is our contention that in many cases they were added wrongly and need to be changed.

Two authors who tried to be sensitive to the usages of "spirit" *(pneuma)* were E.W. Bullinger and V.P. Wierwille. In his book, *The Giver And His Gifts,* Bullinger showed a number of the uses of *pneuma* that the reader of Scripture must recognize. These include God, Jesus Christ, operations and gifts of the *pneuma,* the new nature that is born in the Christian, the nature of man, the character of man, angels, evil spirits, the resurrected body, etc. Wierwille recognized many of these, and although he differs somewhat from Bullinger, as is apparent from studying his book, *Receiving The Holy Spirit Today,* there is a large area of agreement between them. A study of both of these works can be helpful to see the intricacies in this area of study. [13]

---

13. You will not have to read far in this book to realize that we, the authors, do not believe in the "Trinity," at least as it is usually defined by orthodox theologians. We do believe there is God the Father, Christ the Son, and holy spirit. It concerns us that some Christians would, for that reason, discard everything we write in this book. We would ask those Christians to read prayerfully. Bullinger was an orthodox Trinitarian, and a linguist, and he saw clearly the difference between Holy Spirit and holy spirit.

In their works, or in your own study of the subject, you will see that when the words *pneuma hagion* (holy spirit) appear with the article "the," they almost always refer to the *Giver*. You will see also that when *pneuma hagion* appears without an article, as it does about 50 times, it almost always refers to the *gift* of the divine nature. [14]

As we stated, God made Jesus rich by raising Him from the dead and exalting Him as Lord, the heir of all things. That is why the Lord is rich unto all who call upon Him, and why He can give each person a precious gift. In John 5, Jesus spoke prophetically about what He would do after His resurrection:

John 5:19-21,26

Jesus gave them this answer: "I tell you the truth, the Son can do nothing by himself; he can do only what he sees his Father doing, because whatever the Father does the Son also does.

For the Father loves the Son and shows him all he does. Yes, to your amazement he will show him even greater things than these.

For just as the Father raises the dead and gives them life, even so the Son gives life to whom he is pleased to give it.

For as the Father has life in himself, so he has granted the Son to have life in himself.

As Peter said in his Pentecost discourse, it is the exalted Lord Jesus, the Christ, who gives us the gift of holy spirit that He Himself received from His Father, God. [15]

---

14. E.W. Bullinger, *The Giver and the Gift* (Kregel Publications, Grand Rapids MI, 1979); *The Companion Bible*, Appendix 101; Victor Paul Wierwille, *Receiving The Holy Spirit Today* (American Christian Press, New Knoxville OH, 1967). The "rule of thumb" that seems clear in Scripture is that whenever holy spirit is referred to as "given," "filling," "falling upon" or as the element of baptism, it is *pneuma* or *pneuma hagion*, the gift.

---

15. In the sense that every Christian has received from the Lord Jesus Christ exactly the same gift that He first gave to those on the Day of Pentecost, every Christian is a "Pentecostal." Today this term is primarily used to distinguish particular groups of Christians who believe in speaking in tongues.

Acts 2:32,33,38

God has raised this Jesus to life, and we are all witnesses of the fact.

Exalted to the right hand of God, he has received from the Father the promised holy spirit and has poured out what you now see and hear...

Peter replied, "Repent and be baptized, every one of you, in the name of Jesus Christ for the forgiveness of your sins. And you will receive the gift of the Holy Spirit [no article; read "of holy spirit"].

In these verses, we see the "God-to-Christ-to-us" pattern by which we in the Church receive all spiritual blessings. The greatest spiritual blessing anyone can receive is "the gift of holy spirit," the "divine nature" of God that He imparted to Christ and now, via Christ, imparts to all those who make Jesus their Lord.

Before his death, Jesus Christ spoke to His apostles about the "Comforter," the holy spirit that He was going to send them after His ascension. Later, between His resurrection and His ascension, Jesus spent forty days instructing His disciples, and much of what He said to them was regarding the gift of holy spirit He was going to give them soon after His ascension. As recorded in the Gospel of Luke, He gave them some very specific instructions:

Luke 24:49

I am going to send you what my Father has promised; but stay in the city until you have been CLOTHED WITH POWER FROM ON HIGH.

Still later on during those forty days, Jesus referred back to His above statement about the impending blessing coming upon His disciples: The following verses from the Book of Acts were also written by Luke:

Acts 1:1-4

In my former book [the gospel of Luke], Theophilus, I wrote about all that Jesus began to do and to teach until the day he was taken up to heaven, after giving instructions through the Holy Spirit [no article; read "through holy spirit"] to the apostles he had chosen.

After his suffering, he showed himself to these men and gave many convincing proofs that he was alive. He appeared to them over a period of forty days and spoke about the kingdom of God.

On one occasion, while he was eating with them, he gave them this command: "Do not leave Jerusalem, but wait for THE GIFT MY FATHER PROMISED, which you have heard me speak about.

Here Jesus spoke to His disciples about "the gift my Father promised" as synonymous with being "clothed with power from on high" that He had previously told them about. He then goes on to add a third synonymous term:

Acts 1:5

For John baptized you with water, but in a few days you will be BAPTIZED WITH THE HOLY SPIRIT [no article; read "with holy spirit"].

There is a commonly recognized mathematical axiom that things equal to the same thing are equal to each other. It is plain that to be "baptized with the holy spirit," to be "clothed with power from on high" and receiving "the gift" promised by God are all referring to what was first given on the Day of Pentecost and is still given to each person who believes in Jesus Christ as Lord. Furthermore, a brief look at the Greek word for "clothed" (Luke 24:49) will show you that "clothed with power from on high" *equals* "the gift my Father promised" *equals* "baptized with the holy spirit" *equals* "receiving the divine nature and righteousness of God" *equals* being "born again." If $A=B$ and $B=C$ and $C=D$ and $D=E$ and $E=F$, then $A=B=C=D=E=F$. At this point, it is imperative that we see that *each of the above terms refers to what happens to a person at the moment of his new birth.*

See You In (The) Church

The question to be asked now is *when* was the promise that the gift of holy spirit would first be given fulfilled? "May we have the envelope, please? And the answer is..."

Acts 2:1-4

When the day of Pentecost came, they were all together in one place.

Suddenly a sound like the blowing of a violent wind came from heaven and filled the whole house where they were sitting.

They saw what seemed to be tongues of fire that separated and came to rest on each of them.

All of them were filled with the Holy Spirit [no article; read "with holy spirit"] and began to speak in other tongues as the Spirit enabled them.

Scripture is very clear that it was on the day of Pentecost when people were first filled with holy spirit. Here, "filled" is used in regard to the initial outpouring of holy spirit and the simultaneous "filling" of the first believers ever to be born of God. The word "filled" also indicates them *manifesting* holy spirit by speaking in tongues. How do we know that this and all the other terms we have seen refer to *every person* who has, since Pentecost, made Jesus Christ his Lord? See if the following few sections of Scripture put the answer together for you:

Ephesians 1:13,14

And you also were included in Christ WHEN YOU HEARD the word of truth, the gospel of your salvation. Having believed, YOU WERE MARKED IN HIM WITH A SEAL, THE PROMISED HOLY SPIRIT [read "holy spirit"], who [which] is a deposit guaranteeing our inheritance until the redemption of those who are God's possession— to the praise of his glory.

These two verses make it clear that *everyone* who has believed in the exalted Christ as Lord has been signed ("marked"), sealed and delivered. Amen! Each has been given the gift of holy spirit as a deposit guaranteeing his life in the age to come. Following the related nouns and pronouns through Ephesians Chapter One brings us to the last two verses, which show believers in Christ designated as both "the Church" and "the Body of Christ."

Ephesians 1:22,23

And God placed all things under his feet and appointed him
to be head over everything for the church,which is his body,
the fullness of him who fills everything in every way.

Here are two more verses that help to clarify the answer to
when holy spirit was first given:

I Corinthians 12:12,13

The body is a unit, though it is made up of many parts; and
though all its parts are many, they form one body. So it is
with Christ.

For we were all baptized by one Spirit [16] into one body—
whether Jews or Greeks, slave or free— and we were all
given the one Spirit [no article; read "given one spirit"] to
drink.

Certainly it was first available to become a member of the "one
body" *only* when it was first available to be "baptized with [the] one
spirit," which, by the way, is the "one baptism" referred to in
Ephesians 4:5. No occasion fits the requirements except the Day of
Pentecost (Acts 2:1ff). Thus we see that while the phrase "baptized
with holy spirit" is indeed scriptural, it refers specifically to the
moment of a person's new birth, as evidenced by its benchmark
usage regarding the first time this ever happened to anyone.

No one can receive what is not available. The gift of holy spirit,
born in a person as "incorruptible seed," was not available until
Jesus Christ had lived, died, been resurrected, ascended and been
exalted as "Lord." Only then could He give holy spirit to others,
which He first did on the Jewish holiday of Pentecost, as recorded
in Acts Chapter Two.

Some people say, however, that Nicodemus got born again in
John, Chapter Three. Not only does it not say anything like that in
John (Jesus never answered Nicodemus' question in verse nine
about how to be born again), but an overview of Scripture clearly

---

16. The Greek text reads *en heni pneumati,* which can be translated either "with
one spirit" or "by one spirit." Therefore, this phrase can be understood to mean that
we are baptized *with* one spirit—the gift (see Acts 1:8) or baptized *by* one Spirit—
Jesus Christ (who is occasionally referred to as "the Spirit, e.g., II Corinthians
3:17,18).

shows that the new birth was impossible until Jesus fulfilled the prerequisites listed in the above paragraph.

It is important to correctly understand that *if* Jesus' reference to being born again in John 3:3 referred to the same new birth that became available on Pentecost, then He was speaking prophetically about it being available in the future. The reader of God's Word must be sensitive to the changes that occurred on the day of Pentecost pertaining to the gift of holy spirit. In the Old Testament, the spirit was upon only *some* people, and upon them *conditionally* because, like King Saul did, they could lose it. But since Pentecost, every Christian has holy spirit (Acts 2:38; Ephesians 1:13, etc.), and since it is *born* (I Peter 1:23) within, it cannot be lost.

That holy spirit was not given in *birth* until Pentecost is made quite clear in the teaching of the Gospels. The following verses clearly teach that holy spirit was not yet given, and indicate that it would not be given until Jesus was glorified, which was after his death, resurrection, ascension and exaltation as Lord: "Whoever believes in me, as the Scripture has said, streams of living water will flow from within him. By this he meant the Spirit [spirit], whom [which] those who believed in him were later to receive. Up to that time the Spirit [spirit] had not been given, since Jesus had not yet been glorified" (John 7:38,39).

These verses help us understand John 3:3. Note that from Jesus' statement in verse 38, one could easily think that the spirit would be given immediately to anyone who at that time believed in Him. But verse 39 clearly teaches us that holy spirit had not yet been made available and would not be available until after Jesus was glorified. John 3:3 is similar to John 7:38 in that it requires other verses to make clear what Jesus said. God expects us to read and understand each passage of Scripture in the light of all other teaching on the same subject.

There are other verses that show that the change, from holy spirit being given conditionally to being "born" in a person, did not occur while Jesus was on earth. In John 14:17 (which is clearly later than John 3:3), Jesus told the disciples that holy spirit, then "with" them, would later be "in" them. In Luke 24:49, after His death and resurrection, Jesus told the disciples "I am going to send you what my father has promised." Thus it is obvious that the promised holy spirit had not yet been sent in the new birth, even after the resurrection. In Acts 1:4, Jesus told His disciples to "wait" for the gift that had been promised. Then, in verse 8, just before His ascension, Jesus told His disciples that they would have power when holy spirit came on them, so it is clear that even up to just before His ascension into heaven, the gift that Jesus spoke about had still not been given.

The holy spirit is not unique to the New Testament. It was the means by which God empowered His people throughout the Old Testament. In fact, seven of the nine manifestations of holy spirit as listed in I Corinthians 12:8-10 are seen in operation in the Old Testament. Only speaking in tongues and interpretation of tongues are particular to Pentecost and afterward.

There are at least four very significant differences between holy spirit in the Old Testament and the four Gospels (before Pentecost) and in the New Testament (after Pentecost). First, before Pentecost, *God chose* who received holy spirit. There was nothing anyone could do that guaranteed his receiving it. Second, it was given only to some people. Third, God gave the spirit *by measure* so people could do specific jobs. For example, Elisha wanted a "double portion" of the spirit that was on Elijah. Fourth, those who were given the spirit could lose it. For example, Saul received the spirit of God (I Samuel 10:6) to enable him to be the King of Israel, but he later lost it (I Samuel 16:14). David was also given the spirit of God and, after his sin with Bathsheba, prayed that it would not be taken from him (Psalm 51:11).

After Pentecost, however, the choice is no longer God's, but each person's. The gift of holy spirit is readily available to *anyone*. Whoever chooses to believe in Christ as Lord receives holy spirit. Since Pentecost, Jesus Christ, who received holy spirit "without measure," gives it *without measure* forever to all who believe in Him. There is no record in Scripture of anyone after Pentecost losing his holy spirit, because since then it has been *born* within each believer. From that day until today, "everyone who calls on the name of the Lord" receives the same gift and enablements. We will see that radiant Christian living is a matter of knowing what you have and how to use it.

Chapter 2

Your
Liquid Asset

One Baptism

Throughout Scripture, water is a "type" of the holy spirit, that is, water often analogously represents the spirit of God. In fact, in Jeremiah 2:13, God even refers to Himself as a "fountain of living waters" (see also Isaiah 44:3,4). Consider these verses:

John 4:13,14

Jesus answered, "Everyone who drinks this water will be thirsty again, but whoever drinks the water I give him will never thirst. Indeed, the water I give him will become in him a spring of water welling up to eternal life [life in the age to come]."

We saw in Acts 2:33 that Jesus Christ "poured out" the gift of holy spirit. This figurative language, comparing the gift of holy spirit to liquid, reinforces the analogy that we will follow in Scripture for most of this chapter. It is one that will help us understand what happens within each person when he is born again.

When John the Baptist came as a forerunner to the Messiah, many people asked him if *he* were the Christ.

Luke 3:16

John answered them all, "I baptize you with water. But one more powerful than I will come, the thongs of whose sandals I am not worthy to untie. He will baptize you with the Holy Spirit [no article; read "with holy spirit"] and with fire.

Many people believe that John the Baptist was the first to baptize in water, but this is clearly not the case. Hebrews 9:10 mentions "various ceremonial washings" in the law, and the Greek word for "washings" is "baptisms." There are other Greek words for washing that God could have easily used, such as *"pluno,"* which is used of inanimate things; *"nipto,"* used of washing or of washing a part of the body; or *"louo,"* which means "to bathe" or "to wash the entire body." Instead, He chose "baptisms" to refer to the Old Testament washings.

A careful reading of the Old Testament will reveal various types of washings. Exodus 30:17-21 mentions the bronze basin that was placed between the door of the Tabernacle and the altar so the priests could wash their hands and feet. According to Exodus 40:12, Aaron and his sons were brought to the Tabernacle and washed with water. When Solomon built the Temple in Jerusalem, he had a basin cast of bronze that was so large the Bible calls it "the Sea." Scholars estimate that it held about twelve thousand gallons of water and, according to II Chronicles 4:6, the priests washed in it.

The Mosaic Law was full of regulations about washing. There were many different things that could happen to a person to make him unclean, and often the Law said the person had to wash in water in order to re-enter the congregation (Cp. Leviticus 14:9; 15:7,8,11,13,21,22,27; 16:26, 28; 17:15,16). In that sense, bathing in water, beside being a sanitary regulation, had some typological significance. The same was true of John's baptism—the water was symbolic of the rinsing off of sin and of one showing desire to enter the congregation of the kingdom of heaven. Also, the Levites were sprinkled with water before they started ministering in the Tabernacle (Numbers 8:5,7). The Law even had a special water of purification that was used in certain cases of uncleanness (e.g., Numbers 19).

By the time of John the Baptist, there were ritual washing pools all over Israel. Today there are many of these pools to see in the archaeological excavations around Israel, with good examples at Qumran, New Testament Jericho and in Jerusalem itself. It is believed that the Jews of the time of Christ required a new convert to be water baptized. Hasting's *Dictionary of the Bible* says, "a stranger who desired to become a Proselyte of the Covenant, or of Righteousness, i.e., in the fullest sense an Israelite, must be circumcised and baptized, and then offer a sacrifice." It goes on to say that the person was taken "to a pool, in which he stood up to his neck in water, while the great commandments of the Law were recited to him. These he promised to keep. Then a benediction was pronounced and he plunged beneath the water, taking care to be entirely submerged." [17]

The fact that ceremonial and symbolic washing was very familiar to the Jews explains why none of them asked John what his

---

17. *A Dictionary of the Bible* (Hendrickson Publishers, Peabody, MA, originally published by T.&T. Clark, Edinburgh, 1898, reprinted in 1988), James Hastings, "Baptism", Vol. 1, page 239.

baptism meant. Had the ritual been unknown before John, this would have been a logical question. Also, when the priests and Levites came to question John (John 1:19-27), they did not act surprised, as if baptism were a new ritual.

All of these ritual and ceremonial washings of the Old Testament, which were symbolic in nature and pointed to the greater reality of the baptism of holy spirit, were done away with when the reality of the baptism in holy spirit came on the day of Pentecost.

It was John the Baptist who introduced the phrase "baptize with holy spirit." The Greek word *baptizo* means to immerse or to dip. The liquid connotation of "baptizing in holy spirit" must be figurative, because holy spirit is intangible, and cannot literally be poured out, nor can one literally be immersed in it. It is very significant that Jesus Himself was baptized by John, and that at the inauguration of Jesus' ministry, God anointed His Son with holy spirit without measure (John 3:34), which descended in the bodily form of a dove. Accompanying it was a voice from heaven that confirmed to Jesus His sonship, and encouraged Him at this, the start of His ministry.

It is also very noteworthy that the words God spoke when He anointed Jesus with holy spirit confirmed Jesus' sonship. This is one of the parallels between God giving holy spirit to Jesus Christ and Jesus Christ giving it to us. Consider the following verses:

Romans 8:15,16

For you did not receive a spirit that makes you a slave again to fear, but you received the Spirit of sonship [no article; read "spirit"]. And by him [it] we cry, "Abba, Father."

The Spirit himself ["itself"] testifies with our spirit that we are God's children.

The gift of holy spirit is the Christian's proof that he is forever a son of God (Chapter Three will elaborate upon this truth).

The dove and the voice from heaven were phenomena (see Appendix One) designed to mark the significance of this monumental event (Jesus *receiving* holy spirit), just as the phenomena on the Day of Pentecost—the cloven tongues like fire and the sound from heaven like a rushing wind—marked the significance of Jesus Christ first *giving* holy spirit to men. It is important to note that John the Baptist's statement in Luke 3:16 tied together both of these events.

Let us now consider some of the parallels between John's water baptism and Jesus' holy spirit baptism. John's ministry of water baptism followed in the tradition of "various ceremonial washings" prescribed under the Old Testament law (see Hebrews 9:10). Hebrews also tells us, however, that such "fleshly ordinances" were only a "shadow" of better things to come, and that as such they could not "purge one's conscience from dead works" (i.e., change him from the inside out). Luke 3:16 makes it plain that even John the Baptist understood that his water baptism was a "type" of Jesus Christ's holy spirit baptism that was to follow and, by virtue of its infinitely greater power to touch the human heart, to supersede the ceremonial outer cleansing with water. There is no comparison between *water on* and *holy spirit in.*

Jesus Christ corroborated this truth in His instructions to His disciples between His resurrection and His ascension.

Acts 1:4,5

On one occasion, while he was eating with them, he gave them this command: "Do not leave Jerusalem, but wait for the gift my Father promised, which you have heard me speak about.

For John baptized with water, but in a few days you will be baptized with the Holy Spirit [no article; read "holy spirit"]."

As we saw in Chapter One, "the promise of the Father" was that they would be "baptized with holy spirit." A very important word in verse five is "but." This contrasting conjunction juxtaposes what precedes it with what follows it. What Jesus told his apostles was that something much better than water was about to be made available.

As we saw earlier, this holy spirit baptism originated on the Day of Pentecost as recorded in Acts, Chapter Two. I Corinthians 12:13 says that "we were ALL BAPTIZED by one Spirit [spirit] into one body... and we were ALL given the one Spirit [spirit]." The first time anyone was baptized in holy spirit was on Pentecost, and since then the Lord Jesus has "poured out" His spirit upon each person who has done what Romans 10:9 says. Along this line, consider the following verses.

Ephesians 4:4-6

There is one body and one Spirit ["spirit"]—just as you were called to one hope when you were called—one Lord, one faith, one baptism; one God and Father of all, who is over all and through all and in all.

What is the "one baptism" referred to in verse five? Is it John's water baptism, or is it the baptism with the "one spirit" in verse four? It cannot be both, because God's Word plainly states that for the Church, the Body of Christ, Christians, there is only *one baptism*. Clearly, this one baptism is the baptism with holy spirit, in which each person is immersed at the moment he is born again. The following verses illustrate this truth:

Colossians 2:11,12

In him you were also circumcised, in the putting off of the sinful nature, not with a circumcision done by the hands of men but with the circumcision done by Christ,having been buried with him in baptism and raised with him through your faith in the power of God, who raised him from the dead.

Here we see an obvious parallel. Just as the "circumcision" in verse 11 is specifically defined as being spiritual and figurative rather than physical and literal, so the "baptism" in verse 12 is spiritual and figurative. It is the "one baptism" with holy spirit, not a literal baptism with water.

Despite the clarity of Scripture in showing that the relevance of water baptism has been nullified by the greater baptism of holy spirit, the vast majority of Bible-believing Christians today practice John's old water baptism. Today, many churches place great emphasis on the ritual of water baptism as a demonstration of one's commitment to Christ. The fact is, however, that it is not conformance to any outward ritual that demonstrates true Christian commitment. Haven't we all seen "baptized" people who act like unbelievers? When the truth of God's Word is taught, a Christian can demonstrate his commitment by a faith and practice that is very visible and tangible.

Although we see nothing sinful in the practice of water baptism, it grieves us that many Christians are, in some cases *literally*, being "held under" an obsolete requirement that often obscures the greater reality of God's gracious gift within them. The "both and" attitude toward the two baptisms severely dilutes the "either or" perspective of Scripture toward the *one baptism* and diminishes its vital significance. It is somewhat analogous to being content with kissing your spouse's *shadow* (Hebrews 10:1a).

It is beyond the scope of this book to expound on all the verses related to baptism other than what we have done here. Among them, however, in regard to the weakness of the law, which is where the ceremonial cleansing of water originated, would be Hebrews 7:18,19:

Hebrews 7:18,19

The former regulation is set aside because it was weak and useless (for the law made nothing perfect), and a better hope is introduced, by which we draw near to God.

Another most pertinent verse is I Peter 3:21, which specifically points out that it is *not water* that saves a person, but something powerful enough to touch one's conscience:

I Peter 3:21

And this water SYMBOLIZES baptism that now saves you also—not the removal of dirt from the body [i.e., NOT WATER] but the pledge of a good conscience toward God. It saves you by the resurrection of Jesus Christ.

Yes, there are a few instances in the Book of Acts (after Pentecost) and at least one place in the Church Epistles (I Corinthians 1:14-17) [18] where water is specifically mentioned or implied as the element of baptism. BUT—two things must be noted: First, there was no doctrinal directive to baptize in water, and second, there are many verses that speak of baptism *without mentioning water* (e.g., Matthew 28:19). Most Christians have been taught that such verses automatically refer to water baptism. That this is not the case is clear in the following verses:

---

18. Why Paul baptized the few believers he mentions in I Corinthians, Chapter One, is not stated. Perhaps they were "zealous for the law" (like the Jews in Acts 21:20) and perhaps, like Philip with the eunuch (Acts 8:27ff), Paul determined that since they had already believed in Christ and had thus been baptized in holy spirit, he would go along with the old tradition so as not to offend their weak consciences. The important thing to note in I Corinthians 1:17 is Paul's declaration that "CHRIST SENT ME NOT TO BAPTIZE, but to preach the gospel." Amen.

Romans 6:3

Or don't you know that all of us who were baptized into Christ Jesus were baptized into his death?

I Corinthians 12:13

For we were all baptized by one Spirit into one body—whether Jews or Greeks, slave or free—and we were all given the one Spirit to drink.

Galatians 3:27

For all of you who were baptized into Christ have clothed yourselves with Christ.

These uses of the word "baptized" cannot refer to water, because there is no logical (or biblical) connection between water baptism and salvation. These verses "do not hold water," so we cannot add it to them. What then are they talking about? They are talking about the *one baptism* in holy spirit, synonymous with the new birth, that is, being saved. Almost any Christian would admit that there are "baptized" church members who are not actually saved.

How sad that the Church has so emphasized John's old water baptism and even fought tooth-and-nail about how much water and how it should be administered. For too many Christians, water has, in essence, drowned the greater reality of the baptism with holy spirit that each person receives at the moment he is born again.

We see this over and over. We (the authors) have often been asked by Christians whether we have been baptized in water. In contrast, we have seldom been asked whether we have the power of God in operation in our lives—the clear indicator of our baptism in holy spirit. It is well known today that you cannot join some churches until you have had "John's baptism," but those same churches will accept you with no evidence that you have received the baptism John said Jesus would make available. The Word of God is very clear as to which is the greater reality. Praise God that His wonderful Word has "all things that pertain to life and godliness." Therein we can see the greatness of what we have in Christ, and how we can live accordingly.

Have You Received "The Anointing"?

As stated earlier, "the anointing" is a term many Christians use to describe an additional filling of holy spirit or a temporary spiritual enabling. For example, right after quoting I John 2:27 from *The Amplified Bible,* where it says "...the anointing which you received from Him abides (permanently) in you," one Christian leader goes on to say:

> The anointing is the power of God to destroy every yoke of bondage on your life and on the lives of those to whom you minister. We are anointed (empowered by the Holy Spirit) for specific tasks or callings. For example, I would not dare attempt to teach the Word and minister to people without the anointing.

> You need an anointing to be a wife or a husband, a parent, a friend, a businessperson. It is extremely important in the world we live today that you know how to walk in God's anointing. I honestly believe that you need an anointing to go to the grocery store...if you expect to come out with peace and joy! [19]

Let us restate that we are not challenging the heart of this precious person, but rather the way she and countless other Christians use the word "anointing." Here people are being taught that they need "the anointing" to do just about anything. In the context of what she said, it is easy to see how such teaching could cause people who do not think they have the anointing to be very passive and fearful, and, in this case, leave them unmarried, childless, friendless, jobless...and foodless! This is an extreme example, but it is by no means totally atypical. Our point is that if you are a Christian, you have "the anointing," and you are equipped for *all* situations. Then, as she rightly says, it is up to you to utilize the ability you have and *walk* in God's power.

We are not trying to antagonize Pentecostals and Charismatics who use the word "anointed" in reference to temporary spiritual

---

19. *Joyce Meyer Ministries Newsletter,* by Joyce Meyer, August, 1994.

enablements, and we recognize that there are genuine experiences they are trying to describe. God does work with us as we step out in faith to obey Him. He energizes His gift of holy spirit in His people, resulting in manifestations of power (such as word of knowledge, word of wisdom, faith, miracles and healing) that are just not available for us to do by the flesh alone.

Our point in this book is that Christians have the responsibility to study the words in God's Word and to use the vocabulary of Scripture the way God uses it. Christians will not come to a "unity in the faith and in the knowledge of the Son of God" (Ephesians 4:14) if we do not use the vocabulary of the Word of God the way God does. How are Christians, who come from diverse cultural and denominational backgrounds, going to reach a common under-standing if we use our own denominational jargon and ignore the way the Word of God uses its own vocabulary?

It must be very confusing to a person who constantly hears about "the anointing" as if it were a temporary enabling that occasionally comes upon Christians, and who then reads the Bible and *never* finds the word used that way. In listening to many people talk about "the anointing," we have decided that the biblical equivalent to what they are saying is an *energizing* of the gift of holy spirit that is already within a believer. The word "energize" is used this way in God's Word, as the following verse shows:

I Corinthians 12:6

There are different kinds of working [*energemata*], but the same God works [*energeo*] all of them in all men.

The gift of holy spirit is the "equalizing factor" among all members of the Body of Christ. Each one has the power of God to serve in whatever capacity He is called and directed by the Lord. Obviously, these callings of God are extremely varied, depending upon people's unique desires and abilities, and how God is able to work with them according to their faith.

In this section, we will focus on the word "anoint" as it is actually used in the Word of God. The New Testament Greek verb is *chrio*, which means "to touch the surface of a body slightly, graze; to rub over; to anoint." [20] In the Old Testament, anointing with oil was part of the God-prescribed formula for installation and conse-

---

20. Bullinger's Lexicon, page 54.

cration to an office such as priest or king (see Exodus 28:41; 29:7; 40:13,15; I Samuel 9:16; 16:3,12, 13. Moses actually prescribed a special oil for anointing, as recorded in Exodus 30:22-30).

From the word *chrio* comes *christos*—"the anointed one." We're sure you are making the connection—Jesus "Christ" is more literally Jesus "the Anointed One." This is also the meaning of the word "Messiah," which comes from the Hebrew word for "anoint." Remember that Jesus never wrote "Christ" in the "Last Name" box on any insurance forms. "Christ" is the title He carries and the office He is fulfilling as the Old Testament-promised Messiah (anointed one) who would come to save Israel. As per Acts 2:36, He is Jesus *the* Christ.

Of course, Jesus knew who He was, and at the beginning of His ministry He referred to a prophecy in Isaiah 61:1,2 about Himself. Note the word "anointed."

Luke 4:17-21

The scroll of the prophet Isaiah was handed to him. Unrolling it, he found the place where it is written: The Spirit of the Lord is on me, because he has ANOINTED me to preach good news to the poor. He has sent me to proclaim freedom for the prisoners and recovery of sight for the blind, to release the oppressed, to proclaim the year of the Lord's favor. Then he rolled up the scroll, gave it back to the attendant and sat down. The eyes of everyone in the synagogue were fastened on him, and he began by saying to them, "Today this scripture is fulfilled in your hearing."

It is noteworthy that Jesus quoted this prophecy shortly after God had anointed Him with holy spirit. Let us once again note when this anointing took place:

Luke 3:21, 22

When all the people were being baptized, Jesus was baptized too. And as he was praying, heaven was opened and the holy spirit descended on him in bodily form like a dove. And a voice came from heaven: "You are my Son, whom I love; with you I am well pleased."

In Acts 10, Peter referred back to the days of Jesus' earthly ministry and its powerful effect upon those whose lives He touched.

Acts 10:36-38

You know the message God sent to the people of Israel, telling the good news of peace through Jesus Christ, who is Lord of all.

You know what has happened throughout Judea, beginning in Galilee after the baptism that John preached—how God ANOINTED Jesus of Nazareth with the Holy Spirit [no article—read "holy spirit"] and power, and how he went around doing good and healing all who were under the power of the devil, because God was with him. [21]

At Jesus' baptism, the dove was emblematic of the spirit of God coming upon Him to consecrate and enable Him for His service to God's people. This is consistent with what we see throughout the Old Testament, where God put a measure of His spirit upon people for particular purposes at particular times. John 3:34 tells us that when God anointed Jesus, He did not give Him the spirit "by measure," i.e., God poured out upon His Son all He could give Him. Jesus' anointing was the culmination, and the ultimate example, of God choosing certain believers upon whom to put a measure of His spirit.

Jesus utilized the spirit of God upon Him to do all that was required of Him as the Messiah, including dying on the cross. In His resurrection, ascension and exaltation, the Lord Jesus has been given the ability and the authority to pour out this holy spirit and anoint each person who believes in Him as Lord.

Two verses in Hebrews refer to Psalm 45:6 and 7 and augment the truth about the consummation of Jesus' anointing by God after His exaltation as Lord. Here the Messiah is called "God" according

---

21. The phrase "anointed with the Holy Spirit" is so often used among Christians today that one would think it occurs many times in the Bible. The fact is that it occurs only once, and that is in Acts 10:38. The spirit of God that had come on Jesus after his water baptism by John stayed on Him the rest of His life. There is no record, and no reason to believe, that Jesus was ever "anointed" again. In the Old Testament, a person could be "anointed" with holy spirit more than once because the spirit, not being born in him, could be given and then taken back by God. Samson is the only person recorded in Scripture from whom God took the spirit He had given him and then gave it back to him again, although in that record the word "anoint" is not used.

to the common Hebrew designation of an earthly representative of the One True God: [22]

Hebrews 1:8,9

But about the Son he says, "Your throne, O God, will last for ever and ever, and righteousness will be the scepter of your kingdom. You have loved righteousness and hated wickedness; therefore God, your God, has set you above your companions by ANOINTING you with the oil of joy.

In their prayer in Acts 4:24-30, Peter, John and the other disciples cited this same truth from God's Word to help bolster their faith.

Acts 4:27

Indeed Herod and Pontius Pilate met together with the Gentiles and the people of Israel in this city to conspire against your holy servant Jesus, whom you ANOINTED.

Their reference is to Psalm 2, which in verse two refers to "the Lord and...his anointed [one]." This psalm regards Christ's still future ministry to Israel after his exaltation at the right hand of God.

On the Day of Pentecost, the exalted Lord Jesus began the Church and His ministry to it. As the following verses show, He did so by "pouring out" the gift of holy spirit and thus anointing each believer:

Acts 2:32,33

God has raised this Jesus to life, and we are all witnesses of the fact. Exalted to the right hand of God, he has received from the Father the promised Holy Spirit [read "holy spirit"] and has POURED OUT what you now see and hear.

Since Pentecost, Jesus Christ has "anointed" each person who believes on Him at the moment of the person's new birth. In so doing, He has passed on to us the gift of holy spirit He Himself received from His Father. Now, each and every Christian is an anointed minister of the Gospel with the power to walk in the steps of the Lord.

---

22. See Appendix Two: The Flexible Usage of "God" and "Lord"

The word "anoint" is used only once in the Church Epistles (Romans through Thessalonians), and this use makes it clear that every Christian is anointed with holy spirit from the moment of his new birth:

II Corinthians 1:18-22

But as surely as God is faithful, our message to you is not "Yes" and "No." For the Son of God, Jesus Christ, who was preached among you by me and Silas and Timothy, was not "Yes" and "No," but in him it has always been "Yes." For no matter how many promises God has made, they are "Yes" in Christ. And so through Him the "Amen" is spoken by us and you stand firm in Christ. He ANOINTED us, set his seal of ownership on us, and put his Spirit ["spirit"] in our hearts as a deposit, guaranteeing what is to come.

Verse 21 makes it very clear that each and every Christian has "the anointing." Note the past tenses of "anointed," "set his seal" and "put his spirit." These are accomplished realities. Each Christian is equipped for service today and is sealed with the guarantee of everlasting life in the age to come.

This anointing—the gift of holy spirit—is also practically relevant to our lives today. As our perfect connection to the Head, Jesus Christ, it gives us the ability to separate truth from error, as the following verses show:

I John 2:24-27 (*Amplified Bible*)

As for you, keep in your hearts what you have heard from the beginning. If what you heard from the first dwells *and* remains in you, then you will dwell in the Son and in the Father (always),

And this is what He Himself has promised us, the life, the eternal [life].

I write this to you with reference to those who would deceive you—seduce and lead you astray;

But as for you, (the sacred appointment, the unction) the anointing which you received from Him, abides (permanently) in you; [so] then you have no need that any one should instruct you. But just as His anointing teaches you concerning everything, and is true, and is no falsehood, so you must abide—live, never to depart [rooted in Him, knit to Him] just as [His anointing] has taught you [to do]. [23]

The heart of each Christian is filled to overflowing with all that is contained in the gift of holy spirit with which each has been forever anointed. God's love, joy and peace are within us. Through His Son Jesus Christ, our Heavenly Father has called us, consecrated us and empowered us for a life of joyful service to Him. At the moment he gave us life, He gave us all we will ever need to live it. Let us do so for His glory.

Filled To Overflowing

As we move along in this chapter dealing with "our liquid asset," we now want to consider the third phrase that many Christians are misusing, as mentioned in our Introduction. The term "filled with (or full of) the holy spirit" is being used to teach that Christians can receive more holy spirit than they were filled with when they were born again. In all fairness, there are Scripture verses that do seem to indicate this, and it is these we want to address. Before we examine them, let us look at two verses that make it very clear that one receives holy spirit when he believes, that is, at the time of his salvation and new birth:

Ephesians 1:13,14

And you also were included in Christ when you heard the word of truth, the gospel of your salvation. Having believed, you were marked in him with a seal, the promised Holy Spirit [holy spirit], who [which] is a deposit guaranteeing our inheritance until the redemption of those who are God's possession—to the praise of his glory.

---

23. Sometimes you hear people quote verse 27a to defend the obvious error that "the Holy Spirit" will teach you all you need to know, independent of the written Word of God. Why then would there be "teachers" set by Christ in the Church (Ephesians 4:11)? In context, the above verses are speaking of counterfeit "believers" teaching doctrinal error about Jesus Christ among true believers. John is saying that Christians should listen to the spirit of God within them rather than to such false teachers. We know that the spirit of God never contradicts the written Word of God, which should remain in our hearts as the ultimate standard for truth (Hebrews 4:12).

We believe that it borders on blasphemy to teach that when a person is born again, he receives only a part of the spirit and that the Lord will keep giving more holy spirit to him as he lives his Christian life. Ephesians 1:3 says that the Christian has "EVERY spiritual blessing." Colossians 2:10 says that the Christian is "complete." Such verses make it clear that at the time of his new birth, the Christian is given all the spirit he or she is ever going to receive from the Lord.

We will see that the phrase, "filled with the holy spirit" is used by God to indicate an *overflowing into evidence.* The first use of this phrase is in Acts 2:4, regarding the initial outpouring of holy spirit on the Day of Pentecost. Remember that the apostles saw tongues like fire "rest" upon each other and they heard the rushing mighty wind. These signs showed them that they had received within themselves the "promise of the Father" that Jesus had told them about. These signs were not totally unexpected. John the Baptist had said that the Messiah would baptize with "holy spirit and fire" (Matthew 3:11; Luke 3:16). Also, between His resurrection and the day of Pentecost, and shortly before His ascension, Jesus had appeared to the apostles, "breathed on them and said, 'Receive the holy spirit'" (John 20:22). When Jesus breathed on them, the sound would have been very similar to wind, the same sound you make when you breathe out. So, hearing the wind and seeing the fire on the day of Pentecost, the apostles realized that the gift of holy spirit they were waiting for had been given. The evidence that they had been filled with holy spirit was that they spoke in tongues.

We will see that in each case where the phrase "filled with the holy spirit" is used, those referred to already have received the gift of holy spirit, and are not receiving more spirit. Rather, they are utilizing outwardly what they have been given inwardly. It is not "an empty" vessel being filled or a leaking vessel being refilled, but a "full" vessel overflowing.

We will focus on three Greek words translated "filled" and "full"— *pleres, pletho* and *pleroo*—and study their individual and overlapping usages. In so doing, we will see that it is primarily the context in which they appear that determines whether they mean filled *to capacity* with holy spirit or filled *to overflowing.* By "overflowing," we mean where the person "filled" *manifests* the gift of holy spirit within him in an evident way, that is, there is specific action on his part in response to the spirit working in him.

Inherent in the term "filled" is the idea of a container, which can be empty, partly filled, completely filled or filled to overflowing. With regard to being filled with holy spirit, the question to ask is, "What determines our capacity and the amount we receive?" We saw in John 3:34 that Jesus Christ received the holy spirit "without measure" (i.e, to the fullest capacity). Anointed with this spirit of power, he was enabled to do His Messianic works (Acts 10:38). John 14:12 indicates that all those who believe in Christ will be similarly enabled to do the works that He did (and greater works), which they could do only if they are given the same amount of holy spirit, that is, also without measure.

Therefore, the "measure" of holy spirit one is given at the moment of his new birth is the same measure that Jesus Christ received. He is our standard. Scripture records that it was indeed Christ, at Pentecost, who "poured out" upon his disciples this promised "liquid asset" He had received from His Father (Acts 2:33). He filled them to capacity, thus enabling them to do the works that He did. If the amount of holy spirit we receive were dependent upon and in accordance with our faith or capacity to believe, there would be a vast diversity among Christians in the amounts of holy spirit they have. Thankfully, this is not the case. Again, the measure of holy spirit each Christian receives has been determined by the work and ministry of Jesus Christ.

It is common knowledge that Luke penned both his own gospel and the Book of Acts. In his writings, *pleres* and *pletho* are often used interchangeably. The first use of *pleres* is in Luke 4:1, where it describes Jesus as being "full [*pleres*] of holy spirit," and led into the wilderness. This happened shortly after He received holy spirit when He was baptized by John the Baptist. This reference to Christ being led by God indicates more than a filling to capacity, and in essence means an overflowing into manifestation (action).

In Acts 6:3, the apostles exhorted the disciples to look for seven men "full [*pleres*] of spirit and wisdom." If all the believers had already been filled with holy spirit when they were born again, why look for some specific men who were "full?" This must be a reference to actions evident in their lives that were perceivable to those choosing them.

Stephen is chosen as one of these seven, and is described as "full [*pleres*] of faith and of holy spirit" (Acts 6:5). When Stephen saw the glory of God and beheld Jesus standing on the right hand of God (Acts 7:55), he is again described as being "full [*pleres*] of holy spirit." Obviously, something more is meant in these phrases than the fact that Stephen was born again and therefore "full" of holy spirit. In the latter context, it is clear that he was inspired and had a spiritual experience, a vision that came to him by way of holy spirit within him.

Another verse in which *pleres* is used is Acts 11:24, where Barnabas is described as "full [*pleres*] of the Holy Spirit [no article; read 'of holy spirit'] and of faith." This is another reference to the fact that Barnabas was one who *walked* by the spirit, not just that he had it within him. This fact is borne out by the description of Barnabas in Acts 13 and 14.

The above uses of *pleres* are plainly analogous to the predominant usage of the word *pletho* in the following verses, which also indicate a state of inspiration in which a specific action follows one's being "filled":

Luke 1:41

Elizabeth was filled [*pletho*] with the Holy Spirit [no article; read "with holy spirit"]. In a loud voice she EXCLAIMED...

Luke 1:67

Zachariah was filled [*pletho*] with the Holy Spirit [no article; read "with holy spirit"] and PROPHESIED...

Acts 2:4

And they were all filled [*pletho*] with the Holy Spirit [no article; read "with holy spirit"] and BEGAN TO SPEAK IN OTHER TONGUES...

Acts 4:8

Then Peter, filled [*pletho*] with the Holy Spirit [no article; read "with holy spirit"], SAID to them [the rulers who stood against him]...

Acts 4:31

...and they were all filled [*pletho*] with the Holy Spirit [no article; read "holy spirit"], and they SPOKE the Word of God boldly...

In regard to Acts 4:31, verse 23 of Chapter Four indicates that the apostles returned to "their own people" and reported to them, prayed with one accord, etc. This was an assembly of believers, so they were already "full of holy spirit," but they are described this way in verse 31 because they were inspired and then manifested holy spirit. They also experienced a phenomenon—the place where they were was shaken.

In Acts 13:9, Paul confronted Elymas the sorcerer and, being "filled [*pletho*] with the Holy Spirit [no article; read 'with holy spirit']," received revelation about Elymas' devilish purposes and spoke by the spirit to invoke the power of God to thwart him. Here we see another clear illustration where to be "filled with holy spirit" means to put this power into practice.

Outside of Luke's writings, there are only three uses of *pletho* in the New Testament: Matthew 22:10 (the wedding hall "filled" with guests); Matthew 27:48 and John 19:29 (the sponge "filled" with vinegar). These verses support the dominant meaning of *pletho* as "filled to overflowing."

There is another Greek word relevant to this issue, and it is found in Ephesians 5:18: "Be not drunk with wine...but be filled [*pleroo*] with the Spirit [no article; read 'with spirit']." Some have thought of this as an exhortation to the unsaved, but why would this be found in Scripture addressed to "the saints" and "the faithful" who have already been blessed with all spiritual blessings (Ephesians 1:3), and who have been "sealed with the holy spirit" (Ephesians 1:13)? Also, it is in an immediate context in which those being addressed are called "light in the Lord" (Ephesians 5:8).

Why is the imperative command, "be filled," given to those who are already filled with holy spirit? This must refer to *action* that can be taken by the believer, or it could not be commanded. Clearly, *pleroo* (like *pleres* and *pletho*) is used here in the sense of being filled to overflowing, or into manifestation. It is not up to God to give us more spirit, it is up to us to walk by the spirit He has already given us, and to *move out* as His spirit *moves in* us. Indeed, God cannot fill us again, because He has "sealed" us. If God has sealed something, it can't leak out!

Thus it is clear that Scripture makes a distinction between the filling God does at one's new birth and a particular "filling" into manifestation that is "energized" by God and "activated" by the renewed-mind obedience of the believer. In studying the biblical uses of the phrase, "filled with the spirit," we believe it is important to grasp that it refers not to a *filling up* of holy spirit, but to an *overflowing*. The difference is very important. A Christian need not ask for holy spirit. Rather, he is to utilize the holy spirit he already has, bringing it into powerful external evidence.

This is not what it is commonly taught, however. It seems that many Christians believe they are to be given something they do not have, rather than having what they do have be energized so that it overflows into manifestation. Isn't the latter concept much more appealing and encouraging? Biblical truth cannot be improved upon by theological opinion, no matter how sincere.

WHY SO MUCH CONFUSION?

The great truth of the Giver and the gift (see Chapter One) is very difficult to apprehend for someone who believes in the traditional teaching referred to as "the Trinity." [24] Although many Christians persist in using this term, it is not found in Scripture, as freely admitted by Trinitarians themselves. Let us allow the very Trinitarian *New Bible Dictionary* to enlighten us about this doctine:

> In most formularies the doctrine is stated by saying that God is One in His essential being, but that in this being there are three Persons, yet so as not to form separate and distinct individuals. They are three modes or forms in which the divine essence exists. 'Person' is, however, an imperfect expression of the truth inasmuch as the term denotes to us a separate rational and moral individual. But in the being of God there are not three individuals, but only three personal self-distinctions within the one divine essence. Then again, personality in man implies independence of will, actions, and feelings, leading to behavior peculiar to the person. This cannot be thought of in connection with the Trinity:

---

24. One Trinitarian scholar who did recognize this delineation was E.W. Bullinger, whose book, *The Giver And His Gifts,* is footnoted in this book.

each Person is self-conscious and self-directing, yet never acting independently or in opposition. When we say that God is a Unity, we mean that, though God is in Himself a threefold centre of life, His life is not split into three. He is one in essence, in personality and in will. When we say that God is a Trinity in Unity we mean that there is unity in diversity, and that diversity manifests itself in Persons, in characteristics and in operations. Moreover, the subsistence and operations of the three Persons are marked by a certain order, involving a certain subordination in relation, though not in nature. The Father as the fount of deity is First: He is said to originate. The Son, eternally begotten of the Father, is Second: He is said to reveal. The Spirit, eternally proceeding from the Father and the Son, is Third: He is said to execute. While this does not suggest priority in time or in dignity, since all three Persons are divine and eternal, it does suggest an order of precedence in operation and revelation. Thus we can say that creation is from the Father, through the Son, by the Holy Spirit. [25]

Is it just us, or does this definition confuse you too? The point we want to make in this book is that this incomprehensible, inexplicable and unbiblical dogma has harmful consequences in practical Christian living, not the least among which is confusion about "the holy spirit." This issues in a strong tendency not to utilize the gift of holy spirit one has been given, but rather to wait for a "Third Person" to control him and "use" him.

The Bible is, essentially, the record of two men—the "first Adam" and "the last Adam" (I Corinthians 15:45). The Hebrew word *adam* means "man." The first Adam disobeyed God, received the seeds of death and then, before he died, produced a race of dead men (Romans 5:12). In direct contrast, the last Adam obeyed God all the way to the death of the cross, lived via resurrection and will produce a race of people who will live forever with Him in a restored Paradise.

Scripture clearly states (Romans 5:12-21) that since it was a man who sinned and died, only another man could redeem mankind, and to do so he would have to both live a sinless life and

---

25. *The New Bible Dictionary* (Wm. B. Eerdmans Publishing Co, Grand Rapids, MI, 1974) page 1300.

conquer death. Jesus Christ was a lamb from out of the flock, but in order to be a sacrifice sufficient for the sin nature *and* the sinful behavior of all men, He had to be a lamb "without spot or blemish," that is, he had to have a sinless nature (like the first Adam). He then had to choose to live a sinless life (unlike the first Adam). By creating a perfect sperm in the womb of a virgin, God made Jesus "the last Adam." Jesus then chose, moment by moment, to obey His heavenly Father even unto the horrible death of the cross.

Because Jesus did so, God made Him perfect through sufferings, raised Him from the dead, highly exalted Him and made Him "Lord." Jesus did not perfect, raise, exalt or make Himself Lord. As the "eldest Son" in God's everlasting family, He will give everlasting life to the "many sons" (Hebrews 2:10) who believed in Him. Jesus Christ has received an inheritance from His Father, and those who believe in Him as "Lord" (Romans 10:9) will share in this inheritance forever.

The above three simple paragraphs capsulize the essence of true Christianity. There is no verse in the Bible that speaks of "the Trinity," "God the Son," "three in one," [26] nor did Jesus ever say, "I am God." If these ideas are the so-called "cornerstone of Christianity," why are they not in Scripture?

The basic truth of Scripture is actually very simple. In contrast to the many "gods" and "lords" in pagan religions (I Corinthians 8:5), the apostle Paul stated that, for the Christian, "there is but one God, the Father, ...and one Lord, Jesus Christ..." Ephesians 4:5,6 says the same thing, that there is "one God" and "one Lord." Jesus Himself stated the same thing while He prayed in Gethsemane shortly before His death: "Now this is eternal life [life in the age to come]: that they may know you, the only true God, and Jesus Christ, whom you have sent" (John 17:3).

In I Timothy 2:4, God tells us that He "wants all men to be saved and come to a knowledge of the truth." What might be the focal point of the truth? The next verse tells us: "For there is one God and

---

26. In I John 5:7b and 8a (*KJV*), the words "...in heaven, the Father, the Word, and the Holy Ghost: and these three are one. And there are three that bear witness in earth..." are not found in *one* of the thousands of Greek manuscripts written before 1500 A.D. They were added sometime later, and there are a number of excellent sources that confirm this. A good one is *A Textual Commentary On The Greek New Testament*, by Bruce M. Metzger (United Bible Societies, New York, 1971) page 715, 716.

one mediator between God and men, the man Christ Jesus." Numbers 23:19 plainly states that "God is not a man..." What is He? John 4:24 says that "God is spirit."

Two things are not identical if there is even one difference between them, right? Consider the following comparison between "the only true God and Jesus Christ whom He sent."

God	Jesus Christ
spirit (John 4:24)	flesh and bone (Luke 24:39)
not a man (Numbers 23:19)	a man (I Timothy 2:5 et al)
Father of Jesus Christ (Ephesians 1:3)	Son of God (John 3:16)
not born (Genesis 1:1)	born of a virgin (Luke 1:31-35)
cannot die (I Timothy 1:17)	died for our sins (I Corinthians 15:3)
cannot be tempted (James 1:13)	tempted in all things like we are (Hebrews 4:15)
knows everything (Isaiah 46:10)	did not know all things (Mark 13:32)
cannot be weary (Isaiah 40:28-31)	weary (John 4:6)

As we said, we cannot set forth in this book all our biblical reasons to oppose the Trinitarian dogma that is capsulized as follows:

The Father is God, the Son is God and the Holy Spirit is God, and together they make One God. They are persons, but not individuals, because they are one. The Son was begotten (i.e., born) of the Father, but eternally born such that the Son and the Father are not only the same age, but the same essential being. The Spirit proceeded from (i.e., came from) the Father and the Son, but came from them such that He did not come from them in time or place but was always actually with the Son.

Another reason to believe that the "Trinity" is an unbiblical, man-made doctrine is the wide range that exists among Trinitarian theologians in their definitions of it. It is so wide that some

Trinitarians actually call other Trinitarians heretics. Although most Christians do not understand the different theological arguments, the fact is that each who says he believes in the "Trinity" must of necessity believe one of the definitions, and this choice by necessity excludes the others. [27]

Most people who say they are trinitarians believe that the "Trinity" is simply God the Father, God the Son and God the Holy Spirit. We believe that if most people really studied the doctrine of the "Trinity" and actually understood what was being stated, many of those who now say "I do not understand it" would say "I do not believe it."

Psalm 12:6 says that the words of God are pure words. God uses the words that men use, but He does not use them haphazardly and imprecisely as men do. We have no right to change the simple definitions of words like "one," "God," "man," etc, etc. If such words mean at all what most everyone knows they mean, then God and His only begotten Son are two entirely distinct beings. No amount of theological doubletalk can make Jesus Christ "God the Son," or mix

---

27. One version of Trinitarian doctrine states that Christ was fully man in a union of natures. Another states that Christ put aside his divinity to take on full manhood. Another version, called "Oneness" or "modalism" [not believed by some to actually be Trinitarian] states that Christ was actually God the Father in another mode of being.

Why all the confusion among Trinitarians themselves? Because the Bible never describes any kind of a "three-in-one" being. What the Bible does speak of is one God—the Father; one mediator and Lord—Jesus Christ the Son; and one gift of God—holy spirit. We, the authors, assert that the vast majority of Christians do not really "believe" in the Trinity since they cannot understand it. Those who say they do really only mentally assent to it, and that because they have been taught it over and over. It seems that few have ever even considered that there may be a rational alternative.

---

28. A thorough explanation of the true relationship between "the only true God and Jesus Christ, whom He has sent" (John 17:3) would be in itself a large book. It is not our purpose here to delve deeply into this massive subject. Anthony Buzzard has done a superb work in his 200-page book, *The Doctrine Of The Trinity: Christianity's Self-Inflicted Wound*, available through Christian Educational Services. CES has a four-tape seminar titled *Jesus Christ: The Diameter Of The Ages*, a tape titled *A New Race For A New Age* and other materials that elaborate on this most-important-of-all biblical subjects. We have also reprinted some excellent works on this subject that were originally written in the seventeenth, eighteenth and nineteenth centuries.

in a "third person" so that "three" equals "one." [28] It is unfortunate that so many Christians think that the same logic, linguistic sense and rational thought they use in everyday life are not applicable to spiritual matters.

WHAT ABOUT "THE HOLY SPIRIT"?

Since "the only true God" is "the Father," and since He is "holy" and He is "spirit," He is also referred to in Scripture as "the Holy Spirit." In Chapter One, we saw the difference between the Giver and His gift. The Giver is God, the only true God, the Father, the Holy Spirit. His gift is incorruptible seed (I Peter 1:23), His own divine nature (II Peter 1:13), holy spirit (Acts 2:39). Jesus expressed this truth in John 3:6: "That which is born of Spirit [God, the giver] is spirit [His nature, the gift]." If there is no such thing as the "Trinity," there is no such thing as "the third Person of the Trinity" known as "the Holy Spirit." Anthony Buzzard and Charles Hunting articulately write about this issue:

> It is going beyond the evidence of Scripture to equate the Spirit of God with a person distinct from the one God, *in the same sense as the Son is distinct from the Father.* There are clear differences between what the Bible says about the Father and the Son and what it says about the Spirit. God and Christ are obviously separate individuals worthy of receiving worship: the Father in His capacity as Creator, the Son Jesus as instrument in the salvation of mankind. Yet the Holy Spirit has no personal name. Why is it that in no text of Scripture is the Holy Spirit worshipped or prayed to? Not once does the Holy Spirit send greetings to the churches. When the Apostles write to their churches, greetings are always sent from two persons, the Father and the Son. It is quite extraordinary that Paul would constantly omit mention of the third person of the Trinity, if he believed him to exist. When he charges Timothy to keep the faith, he speaks in the invisible presence of "God and of Christ and of His chosen angels."

A leading biblical theologian of this century, and prominent member of the Church of England, appears to reject the idea that the Bible presents the spirit as a third person:

To ask whether in the New Testament the spirit is a person in the modern sense of the word would be like asking whether the spirit of Elijah is a person. The Spirit of God is of course personal; it is God's *dunamis* (power) in action. But the Holy Spirit is not a person, existing independently of God; it is a way of speaking about God's personally acting in history, or of the risen Christ's personally acting in the life and witness of the Church. The New Testament (and indeed patristic thought generally) nowhere represents the Spirit, any more than the wisdom of God, as having independent personality.

Luke's careful choice of words in three important passages shows how spirit and power are interchangeable terms: John the Baptist will go as a forerunner before the Messiah "in the spirit and power of Elijah." At the conception of the Son of God, Mary is told that *"holy spirit* [there is no article in the Greek] will come upon you and the *power of the Most High* will overshadow you." When Jesus annnounces the coming of the holy spirit at Pentecost, he states his intention to "send forth the promise of My Father upon you; but you are to stay in the city until you are clothed with *power* from on high." The term "Spirit of God" in one passage is replaced by "the finger of God" in the parallel text. The "finger of God" hardly describes a person. [29]

When one is born again of God's spirit, he does not receive a "Person," but rather the divine nature of God, given to men to transform them into the image of His Son. This gift is referred to in Scripture by a number of synonymous terms, including: "holy spirit", "the spirit", "the spirit of God", "the spirit of Christ", "the spirit of the Lord", "the spirit of truth", "the spirit of Sonship" and "the holy spirit of promise", as well as "the new man" and "the divine nature." None of these suggest that the gift is a person. Such teaching is not only biblically groundless, but also logically incom-

---

29. Anthony Buzzard & Charles F. Hunting, *The Doctrine of the Trinity: Christianity's Self-Inflicted Wound*, (Atlanta Bible College and Restoration Fellowship, Morrow GA, 1994) page 102.

prehensible to the rational human mind. Translators, however, influenced by Trinitarian tradition, have unnecessarily muddied the clear waters of the Word in regard to the gift of holy spirit. As an example, let us once again quote Buzzard and Hunting as they write about John 14:15-18,26. The same understanding they set forth applies to John 15:26;16:7,8,13-15.

> In Jesus' last discourses to his disciples, he speaks of the "comforter" who will come to encourage the faithful after Jesus has been taken to the Father. Since "comforter" (*parakletos*) is a masculine word in Greek, translators who believed in the "third Person of the Trinity" rendered the following pronouns as "he" and "him." The same "comforter" is, however, also "the spirit of the truth." This title hardly suggests a person. If we do not assume the Holy Spirit to be a person distinct from the Father and Son, the texts will be rendered as follows:

> If you love me, you will keep my commandments, and I will ask the Father and He will give you another comforter to remain with you until the [coming] age, the spirit of the truth, which the world cannot receive, because it does not see it or know it [*auto*, neuter agreeing with spirit]. But you know it [*auto*] because it remains with you and will be in you. I will not leave you as orphans, I will come to you...But the comforter, the holy spirit, which the Father will send in my name, it [*ekeinos*, masculine in Greek to agree with *parakletos*, but translated as "he" only if it is assumed a person is meant] will teach you all things and remind you of all things I spoke to you. [30]

In the end of this section, let us reiterate why the distinction between the Giver and the gift is important for practical Christian living. If one understands that he has been given the gift of God's power, and that it is up to him to utilize it, he is more likely to aggressively do so. If, however, he believes that a mystical "Third Person" indwells him, he may very well respectfully wait for this "Person" to do for him what Scripture says is his own responsibility.

Another problem arising from the mistaken idea that "the Holy Spirit" is a separate person than God the Father is the teaching that

---

30. Ibid., page 103,104.

"He" comes and goes in and out of our lives. This leads to people "inviting" "Him" into a meeting, singing songs with words like, "You are welcome in this place," and sometimes even praying for hours to "get into His presence." In reality, each Christian is part of "the habitation of God" (Ephesians 2:22) and, via His holy spirit, both God and His Son are *always* with us (John 17:21).

The materials we have referenced will give you many more details about the broad subject of the relationship between the only true God and His Son Jesus Christ. Unless one uses extra-biblical terminology, he cannot explain either the "Trinity" or the many contradictions in Scripture and in logic that this doctrine brings up. Even if extra-biblical terminology is allowed, the explanation makes no sense.

On the other hand, every verse quoted by Trinitarians to "prove" the "Trinity," or that Jesus is God Almighty, is perfectly understandable within the framework of the original languages of Scripture and the customs and culture of the time, in particular the fervent Jewish belief in "One God." All of the more difficult verses on the subject can be understood in light of the many clear verses in God's Word. In each case, we simply need our understanding enlightened or an error in translation corrected. Praise God that this is available.

Chapter 3

It's Your Move

Walking With God: A Reciprocal Relationship

W alking in the power of holy spirit is one result of heart-to-heart fellowship with God, and this involves a reciprocal relationship between God and each believer. The gift of holy spirit is not an inert "mechanism" that we "operate" solely by our own will. Rather, it is the living presence of God in Christ in us, which, while not another "person" living within us, is not an inanimate object either. It is the "divine nature" of God and Christ, and, if you will, contains what might be described as a pre-programmed genetic code designed to reproduce its own characteristics.

It is we, however, who must choose to activate this inner ability. We must work together as "co-laborers" with God (I Corinthians 3:6-9), allowing Him to inspire us and energize His spirit within us. Consider the following verses:

Philippians 2:12-14

Therefore, my dear friends, as you have always obeyed—not only in my presence, but now much more in my absence—continue to work out your salvation with fear and trembling,for it is God who works in you to will and to act according to his good purpose.

Do everything without complaining or arguing.

Sandwiched between the imperative verbs in verses 12 and 14 ("obey," "work" and "do"—our responsibility) is the fabulous promise that God will work in us ("energize" us) in both our will and our ability to walk in the steps of Christ.

In this reciprocal relationship, the issue of control is central to an accurate and balanced view of the interrelationship between holy spirit and the will of the believer. This is because neither the believer nor the spirit is completely in control. Viewing the spirit as a controlling *person* can lead a believer into both false humility and utter passivity—he does nothing without "the Spirit taking over" and acting upon him. This erroneous perspective can cause him to refuse to accept his own responsibility in his relationship with God as set forth in Scripture.

Some Christians may testify that it has been their experience that "the Spirit" did take them over, but, as we stated earlier, no genuine spiritual experience can contradict the Word of God. "I can do all things through Christ who strengthens me" (Philippians 4:13) is the genuine. "Christ or the Holy Spirit can do all things through me" is the counterfeit. We are to be agents, not channels.

We believe this is a great example of how experience alone can be a poor teacher, and why the Word of God is to be our only rule of faith and practice. There certainly can be times when the Lord moves so powerfully in your life that you feel compelled to act, but this is not guaranteed in Scripture. The Christian is to act in obedience to God whether or not he "feels led." Many Christians testify of times when they have "felt compelled" to pray, but also of times when they prayed just because the Bible said to do so, even though they did not feel like praying. The same is true for studying, witnessing, speaking in tongues, fellowshipping with other Christians, etc.

Many Christians have been schooled to think that unless they have specific guidance from "the Spirit," they are out of line to act. When asked whether they speak in tongues, for example, they are apt to say "I have," rather than "I do." They think they have little or no control over how they manifest holy spirit, believing that "the Holy Spirit" manifests "Himself" through them. The notion that they have already been enabled and now must simply act in faith makes such believers feel uncomfortable, carnal and even blasphemous. Also, they reject any idea of "learning" how to manifest the gift of holy spirit, and this too often leaves them ignorant and ineffective.

On the other hand, viewing holy spirit as only a mechanism, an inert battery or a lifeless source of "potential energy" that must be activated by faith, puts the believer in total control. He very well may view with distrust any experience of God acting powerfully within him by the spirit, which he thinks should be completely under his control. This closes off a Christian to many profound and personal experiences that might result from his allowing the Lord to deeply "move" him. As far as his perspective of his relationship with God is concerned, such erroneous thinking also puts God in a box.

Let us consider our reciprocal relationship with the Lord as a dance—a tango in which the partners must function in split-second cooperation and harmony with one another. Generally, the man leads and the woman follows. In a tango, the woman does not just wait to be thrown around the dance floor. Her "following" involves great independence and self-control. She is not coerced, but rather chooses to execute her role with learned skill.

In the big picture, God always "leads," in that He gave us His Son and the gift of holy spirit. We always follow, in that our actions are to be in response to His initiative as expressed in His written Word or in His personal revelation to us. One can easily see the necessity for "dance partners" to become intimately familiar with one another's moves and abilities. The gift of holy spirit makes possible this heart-to-heart relationship between God (and Christ) and each of His children. Not only can the Lord Jesus "coach" us moment by moment, but He can also energize our obedient responses.

Let us pursue the dance metaphor in relation to the manifestations of holy spirit. For example, God "leads" by saying in His Word, "I want you to speak in tongues." It may feel like He is spinning us away from Him and then asking us to fall back trustingly into His arms. We choose to "follow" by operating the mechanics of speech even though we do not have the words in mind. He then "catches us" by supplying us the words with perfect timing.

Let us consider this tension or "dance" between the active and passive aspects in the believer's relationship to the gift of holy spirit within him, as it is revealed in three particular verses of Scripture. The first shows the active aspect, in which the believer's "operation" of holy spirit is emphasized:

I Corinthians 14:32

And the spirits of the prophets are subject to the prophets.
[31]

This verse is set in the context of an exhortation to proper conduct by prophets in the Church. They are encouraged to recognize that holy spirit within them does not compel them to act, that they are ultimately in control and that they can wait for the appropriate time to speak. They do not have to blurt out a message the instant they receive it. The message they speak for God will be best brought forth in love and consideration for all who are ministering and being ministered to. The spirit of God within will not compel obedience to the extent that one cannot resist it. God is not that desperate. If one prophet refuses to speak for Him, He will raise up another who is willing. God is powerful, resourceful and patient, and He works with His people to engender heartfelt obedience and a true willingness to act upon His leading.

The second verse of Scripture shows the passive aspect of the believer's relationship to holy spirit:

II Peter 1:21

For the prophecy never had its origin in the will of man, but men spoke from God as they were carried along by the Holy Spirit [no article; read "by holy spirit"].

In this context, "the prophecy" is synonymous to "the Scripture," or those writings that were inspired by God. These came not by the will of man, but as "holy men of God" freely subjected their wills to the will of God. These were men who had the spirit of God, and it was that holy spirit that "moved" them to speak and write.

---

31. The word "spirits" is the Greek word *pneuma*. Some people believe that it refers to the gift of holy spirit that is born in each believer. Others say that it refers to the "spirit" of man, i.e., one's will, attitudes and emotions. In either case, because the gift of holy spirit can be utilized either properly or improperly, God here reminds the prophets that they are to govern themselves in obedience to His Word. The challenge to the prophet is to speak just what God wants spoken (not necessarily everything God shows him), and not allow anything to keep him from speaking when it is God's will that he speak. This is a great example of why simply *having* the spirit of God is not enough to live a full and vital Christian life. The believer also needs to learn to recognize the voice of the Lord in order to perfect his or her walk with Him.

In II Peter 1:21, the word "moved" is a form of the Greek word *phero,* which basically means "to bring or to carry." Here it occurs in the passive voice (*pheromenoi*), and means "being carried along." This shows that holy men willing to cooperate with God were acted upon by His power. We see this as comparable to a person deciding to swim with the current or walk in the same direction as a "moving sidewalk" in an airport. Two verses in Acts where *phero* occurs in the passive voice give us insight into the powerful nature of the experience of being "moved" by holy spirit.

Acts 27:15

The ship was caught by the storm and could not head into the wind; so we gave way to it and WERE DRIVEN ALONG.

Acts 27:17

When the men had hoisted it aboard, they passed ropes under the ship itself to hold it together. Fearing that they would run aground on the sandbars of Syrtis, they lowered the sea anchor and let the ship BE DRIVEN ALONG.

The context of these verses includes the mention of a powerful storm called Euroclydon. This storm "caught" the ship, which could not be turned into the wind. They had no choice as to their direction, but they did drop the sea anchor so as to slow down the ship as it was being carried along by the wind.

We see the wind as analogous to the moving of God's spirit in II Peter 1:21. Holy men of God were carried along by His spirit, which inspired them to write what God directed. "By holy spirit" is the Greek phrase *hupo pneumatos. Pneumatos* is in the genitive case, which here indicates agency or the means by which something gets done. The spirit is the "channel," or conduit, by which God inspired His Word to be written. *The holy men were not the channels,* for then they would be completely acted upon, and have no will or choice in the matter. This is an important point, especially because many Christians think and speak of themselves as "channels" for the unstoppable power of God.

The "holy men" were men who had freely given their wills to the service of God. At the time they were inspired to write Scripture, their wills were in submission to God's will. A study of their lives shows that, in most cases, it took them years of training and discipline to learn to submit to His will. Once God chose them to write Scripture, however, they entered into a powerful experience of being moved by holy spirit such that there was no doubt at all in their minds about what they were to write. One can be sure that they viewed this powerful experience not as an abrogation of their freedom of will, but as a profound privilege to work in partnership with God and bring His Word into written form, thereby altering human history.

The following verse contains the same word *phero* and also illustrates the principle of the believer's reciprocal relationship with the Lord. The context is the resurrected Christ telling Peter about the potential of his service to others ("Feed my sheep") once Peter had received the gift of holy spirit.

John 21:18

I tell you the truth, when you were younger you dressed yourself and went where you wanted; but when you are old you will stretch out your hands, and someone else will dress you and lead [*phero*] you where you do not want to go.

We can see in this verse that it was Peter's choice whether or not to "stretch" out in faith. When he did, it would be the spirit of God working in him that would "lead" him (carry him along) to places that he would not choose to go if he were only concerned about "feeding" himself.

Many people have been taught that God will "never overstep our free will," and this is true to a great extent, but not absolutely. All choices are not created equal in their ramifications and consequences. For instance, a man is free to join or not join his nation's army. He has a choice at the point of entry. By entering the army, however, he knowingly limits his choices. As long as he remains in that system, he is required to wear a uniform, report for duty, etc. If he chooses to stop doing what army people are *obligated* to do, there are severe consequences—usually the brig. The man may object to the discipline and refuse to obey, saying that his free will has been taken away. His military superiors are unsympathetic, reminding him that his free will was exercised at the point he chose to enter the army, and that he knew what discipline would be involved in that choice. They thus expect him to keep his word and his commitment.

Similarly, when a man decides to make Jesus Christ his "Lord," it should mean that he will from then on *obey* his new Master. If he understands this, he learns to discipline himself to do those things that he knows God wants him to do. At times, God moves him to act for Him in a way that the man does not like or agree with, but he does it anyway, not because he is forced to do so, but because his sense of commitment, duty and responsibility "compels" him. Is his freedom to choose really compromised? No, because he is acting consistently with his prior choice to obey God and submit his will to God's.

We see the same kind of submission to God's will in the following Scripture verses written by the Apostle Paul:

I Corinthians 9:16, 17 (*RSV*)

For if I preach the gospel, that gives me no ground for boasting. For necessity is laid upon me. Woe to me if I do not preach the gospel!

For if I do this of my own will, I have a reward; but if not of my own will, I am entrusted with a commission.

When he confessed Jesus as "Lord," Paul committed himself as a bondslave to his Master, Jesus Christ. From that point on, having thus educated his conscience, he was not "free" to go against whatever his Master asked him to do.

The third and final verse we want to look at clearly shows both the active and passive aspects of each Christian's reciprocal relationship with the Lord.

Colossians 1:29

To this end I labor, struggling with all his energy, which so powerfully works in me.

Notice that Paul labors and struggles with God's energy that powerfully works in him. This is the paradigm: we labor for Him, energized by the strength He supplies. In the above verse, "powerfully" is the Greek word *dunamis,* from which we get the English word "dynamite." Dynamite is a powerful explosive, but it must be activated by blasting caps to produce kinetic power, that is, power that does work. Similarly, the "dynamos" that generate electricity in a hydroelectric plant are useless unless turned by water.

The gift of holy spirit is *dunamis,* potential power, and it must be activated or "turned" by the faith in action of the person in whom the spirit works. Without activating action, the spirit does no work.

On the other hand, action without being inspired and directed by the spirit may produce work, but not fruitful work in accordance with the will of God.

God has graciously given each of His children the ability to do whatever He asks us to do. Although doing the will of God may require great effort on our parts, it is effort that God energizes. When we strive in our own strength, apart from His working within us, we burn out. We are so strongly emphasizing the reciprocal relationship between God and the believer because finding and maintaining this balance is essential to radiant Christian living.

One Gift, Many Uses

In this section, we will look at a classic example of why we as Christians *must* be certain that when we speak about spiritual matters, we accurately represent what God says in His written Word. For example, we cannot call something a "gift" when God calls it a "manifestation."

When it comes to the gift of holy spirit that every Christian has, and the variety of ways in which that gift can be used, critics might accuse us of being too "picky" in our choice of words. However, we did not choose the words, God did, and we feel safe in using the words God chose in the way He chose to use them. What is at stake is far more than mere intellectual one-upmanship. What is at stake is one's whole relationship with God and with his brethren in Christ.

So what's the big deal? What's the difference between a gift and a manifestation? That's a good question, and it has a good answer. A *gift* is individually given, and you do not have it unless someone gives it to you. A *manifestation* is an evidence, a showing forth of something you already have. For example, red spots on your skin are a manifestation of a measles virus someone gave you as a "gift."

Perhaps the multipurpose "Swiss Army" knife is a better example. These knives usually have two blades, two screwdrivers, a can opener, an awl, scissors, a file, etc. If you receive one multipurpose knife as a gift, you can use (bring into manifestation) any or all of its implements. Similarly, the one gift God gives each believer is holy spirit, which each one can manifest in nine ways.

The theology held by translators of modern versions of the Bible is in large part responsible for the erroneous ways in which Christians use so-called "biblical" terminology. One good thing about the *King James Version* and the *New American Standard Version* is that the translators *italicized* many words that are not in the Hebrew or Greek text, but which they added in an attempt to clarify what a verse says, or make it read more smoothly in English. In some verses, their italicized additions are helpful. [32] In the following verses, however, the italicized additions have introduced grievous error, carrying with it corresponding practical consequences for many Christians.

I Corinthians 12:1 (*KJV*)

Now concerning spiritual *gifts*, brethren, I would not have you ignorant.

I Corinthians 14:1 (*KJV*)

Follow after charity and desire spiritual *gifts*, but rather that ye may prophesy.

I Corinthians 14:12 (*KJV*)

Even so ye, forasmuch as ye are zealous of spiritual *gifts*, seek that ye may excel to the edifying of the church.

In each of the above verses, the word "gifts" has been erroneously added. The word "spiritual" is from the Greek *pneumatikos*, which would be better translated "spiritual matters" or "spiritual things." This, of course, then fits with Chapters 12-14, which are not about spiritual *gifts*, they are about spiritual *matters*, among which are "gifts" (12:4), "administrations" (ministries) (12:5), "operations" (workings) (12:6) and "manifestations" (12:7-10). Consider also the following verse:

I Corinthians 13:2 (*KJV*)

And though I have *the gift of* prophecy, and understand all mysteries and all knowledge; and though I have all faith, so

---

32. Such additions would be even more helpful had there been greater consistency in the use of italics. There are many places where additions to the text are not in italics.

that I could remove mountains, and have not charity, I am nothing.

Notice that the words "the gift of" are in italics, indicating that they have been added to the text. If the translators had just said what God originally said instead of adding their own theology, they would have been right. The addition of the spurious words takes prophecy out of the category of a "manifestation" of the gift of holy spirit that "every man" already has, and makes it an additional gift that believers think they do not have and must wait to receive.

The *New International Version* is among the most popular modern translations of the Bible, and it is typical in its disregard for the text in the above verses we just quoted. There is no Greek word for "gift" in the verse, but the *NIV* starts I Corinthians 12:1 with "Now about spiritual gifts..." Since there are no italics or other indication that the word "gifts" is, in reality, an unwarranted addition, the sincere Christian thinks that Chapters 12-14 are about spiritual gifts. Because there are four verses with the word "gifts" wrongly added, the one *proper* use of "manifestation" in I Corinthians 12:7 is overshadowed. With the help of battalions of Bible teachers reinforcing this error by calling speaking in tongues, prophecy, etc., "*gifts* of the spirit," Christians are too often led down the path toward spiritual passivity, inactivity, frustration and defeat. [33]

How so? Because instead of knowing that he has already been given the gift of holy spirit, and learning how to put it to use via speaking in tongues, etc., a Christian waits for God to give him "the gift of tongues." He may even plead and beg with God, and end up disappointed in God for not answering his prayer. [34]

To further clarify that holy spirit is the *one gift* given to each Christian, and that speaking in tongues, prophecy, etc. are *not* gifts, but *manifestations*, or evidences, of the one gift, let us now examine two pertinent Greek words translated "gift."

One word is *dorea*, which is defined in *Vine's Expository Dictionary of the New Testament* as "a free gift, stressing its gratu-

---

33. See Appendix C: Usages Of "Spirit" In The New Testament.

---

34. If you are a Christian who wants to speak in tongues and exercise other manifestations of holy spirit also, C.E.S. has teaching materials that will help you do so. Descriptions of them are in the back of this book.

itous character." [35] It appears eleven times in the New Testament. In each case it refers to the gift of holy spirit that is the essence of the new birth. Here are some of the verses in which it is found:

Acts 2:38

Peter replied, "Repent and be baptized, every one of you, in the name of Jesus Christ for the forgiveness of your sins. And you will receive the gift [*dorea*] of the Holy Spirit [no article: read "of holy spirit"].

Acts 10:45

The circumcised believers who had come with Peter were astonished that the gift [*dorea*] of the Holy Spirit [read "holy spirit"] had been poured out even on the Gentiles.

II Corinthians 9:15

Thanks be to God for his indescribable gift [*dorea*]!

Ephesians 4:7 (*KJV*)

But unto every one of us is given grace according to the measure of the gift [*dorea*] of Christ.

The other uses of *dorea* as "gift" are found in John 4:10; Acts 8:20, 11:17; Romans 5:15, 17; Ephesians 3:7; Hebrews 6:4.

The other Greek word translated "gift" that we will look at is *charisma*. It has been transliterated into our English word "charisma," which today is generally defined as a special capacity to elicit enthusiastic support from others. For example, we speak of "gifted" leaders as having great "charisma." The Greek word means "favor or kindness that is freely given," and it appears seventeen times in the New Testament. [36] From our study of these occurrences, we have put its uses into five categories:

(1) The gift of holy spirit - 2 (Romans 5:15, 16)

(2) Ways unique to an individual believer that the gift of holy spirit is evidenced in his life other than the nine

---

35. *The Expanded Vine's Expository of New Testament Words*, W.E. Vine (Bethany House Publishers, Minneapolis MN, 1984), pages 486-487.

---

36. E.W. Bullinger, *A Critical Lexicon and Concordance to the English and Greek New Testament*, (Samuel Bagster and Sons, Limited, London, Ninth edition, 1969), page 318.

manifestations - 10 (Romans 1:11; 11:29; 12:6a; I Corinthians 1:7; 12:4, 31; II Corinthians 1:11; I Timothy 4:14; II Timothy 1:6; and I Peter 4:10)

(3) Gifts of healing - 3 (I Corinthians 12:9, 28, 30)

(4) Level of sexual drive- 1 (I Corinthians 7:7) (We're not making this up).

(5) Everlasting life in the age to come - 1 (Romans 6:23)

We are aware that in this section we may seem to be getting very technical. What we need to realize is that although it may seem technical to the English-speaking reader, the message of the text is very clear in the Greek. *Dorea* and *charisma* differ in meaning, and it is only when the English translates both of these words as "gift" that there is a problem. Similarly, in the next section we will try to unravel the problem caused by translating *dechomai* and *lambano,* two different Greek words, by the same English word "receive."

As we stated earlier, these verses make it plain that every Christian is "charismatic." Each one has been graciously "gifted" by God with abundant ability to touch the lives of others. We shudder to think of the countless Christians who have gone to their graves without having known the joy of manifesting the priceless riches of God's magnificent gift within them, and we are again reminded of Jesus' statement that the truth would have made them free. Praise God that we have His wonderful Word to enlighten us about "everything we need for life and godliness" (II Peter 1:3).

Utilizing The Manifestations Of Holy Spirit

One thing that hinders Christians from walking in the fullness of God's power is the teaching that each will have only one, or at most a few, of the "gifts of the spirit." This teaching is supported by a misunderstanding of I Corinthians 12:8-10 (*KJV*), which reads:

> For to one is given by the Spirit the word of wisdom; to another the word of knowledge by the same Spirit; To another faith by the same Spirit; to another the gifts of healing by the same Spirit; To another the working of

miracles; to another prophecy; to another discerning of spirits; to another divers kinds of tongues; to another the interpretation of tongues.

While it is true that at first glance these verses seem to indicate that a person can utilize only one of the manifestations of the spirit, deeper study will reveal that this could not be the correct understanding. First, because we are told in I Corinthians 14:5 that God wants *every Christian* to speak in tongues. God would not tell us to do something we could not do, so it is apparent that every Christian *can* speak in tongues. This same logic applies to the manifestation of prophecy, especially in light of the further information revealed in the same chapter—verses 1,12,24, and 39. That makes two manifestations that every believer is to practice. Want to go for three? Okay, in verses 5,12 and 13, the believer is encouraged to interpret what he speaks in a tongue.

Beside the above truths, the fact that I Corinthians 14 is full of directions as to how and when to operate these manifestations, as well as reproof for operating them wrongly, shows that it is the believer who controls his operation of these manifestations of holy spirit. If God controlled the operation of the spirit in a believer's life, there would be no instructions on when and how to manifest the spirit, because He would always do it right.

Along this same line of thinking, *every believer* is encouraged to get to the point that he or she can hear the voice of the Lord. The Bible refers to what God speaks to us as "word of knowledge," "word of wisdom" and "discerning of spirits." When God speaks and gives information or knowledge, it is a "word of knowledge." A good example would be Joseph interpreting Pharaoh's dream (Genesis 41:25-27). God gave Joseph knowledge about the meaning of the dream: seven years of plenty, then seven years of famine. But what if God had not also shown Joseph what to do to keep the famine from ruining Egypt? We need more than knowledge, we need wisdom also. God calls the wisdom He gives when he speaks to us "word of wisdom." God did give Joseph the word of wisdom, and Joseph told Pharaoh to store up twenty per cent of the crops during the plenteous years for the upcoming famine years (Genesis 41:33-36).

When the revelation knowledge and wisdom given by God concerns the presence or non-presence of evil spirits, He calls it "discerning of spirits." Most every Christian realizes how important it is to hear the voice of the Lord. So there are three more manifestations that every Christian can operate. No one would say, "God will give you knowledge but not wisdom, or wisdom but not knowledge." We must be able to receive from the Lord a word of knowledge, and of wisdom and information about evil spirits. Now we're up to six.

What about the other three manifestations in I Corinthians 12:8-10 that we have not yet mentioned? One is "gifts of healing." Jesus Christ made it plain that healing people is something *all believers* can do. He said, "These signs will accompany those who believe...they will place their hands on sick people and they will get well" (Mark 16: 17 and 18). In the same verses, He said that "those who believe" would cast out demons, which is a "miracle" (Mark 9:39). It is plain from the teaching of Christ Himself that *every believer* is to do miracles. The last manifestation in I Corinthians 12:8-10 to discuss is "faith," but it should go without saying that God wants every Christian to have faith. Scripture goes so far as to teach that "without faith it is impossible to please God" (Hebrews 11:6). Six plus three equals nine.

It should be clear from the above verses that God wants each and every believer to speak in tongues, interpret and prophesy. God also wants every believer to hear His voice as He speaks knowledge, wisdom and discerning of spirits. He also gives every believer power to heal, to do miracles and to have faith.

Why then does God seem to confuse us by using the words "to one" in I Corinthians 12:8-10 as if we were not actually to be doing all of them? We see two possible answers. First, the context (remember that there were no chapter breaks in the original text) regards the meeting of the church. This starts back in I Corinthians 11:17 when Paul says, "your meetings do more harm than good." The context of a meeting can be seen all the way through the end of Chapter Fourteen. There are constant references to behaving decently in an assembly and that no one person is more important than another.

In a Christian meeting, not everyone will do everything. Why does God have to say "If anyone speaks in a tongue, two—or at most three—should speak, one at a time"? God has to tell us how to operate the manifestations properly or we will not know how, and in Corinth they were apparently so excited (or possibly puffed up) about their God-given ability that they all wanted to "get in on the act" in the worship service.

We believe that a second reason for the "to one" phrases in I Corinthians 12:8-10 is that they point to the fact that different believers will have "longsuits" in all of the manifestations. Our experience with the manifestations for more than twenty-five years has shown us that, while every Christian has the God-given ability to manifest all nine of the manifestations, each person will have some manifestations at which he or she really excels. [37]

---

37. Another possibility is that advanced by Wierwille in *Receiving the Holy Spirit Today* (American Christian Press, New Knoxville, Ohio). He says that "to another" refers not to a person, but to "the profit" of the manifestation in verse 7. We think this is a grammatical stretch, but it could explain why a different word for "another" (*heteros*) is used with "faith" and "tongues" than with the others in the list (verses 8-10). *Heteros* means another when only two are involved, where with *allos* there may be more than two (*Companion Bible*, Appendix 124). The profit of tongues involves only two: God, who is thanked well (I Corinthians 14:17), and the believer, who is edified. Faith is also primarily a matter between God and the believer, though its effects may have ramifications for many (Romans 4:11; 14:22).

This section may be an example of a figure of speech called *Amphibologia*, in which the same words may have two or more overlapping meanings. See E.W. Bullinger's *Figures of Speech Used in the Bible*, footnote on page 71 after first whole paragraph ending "God and His Son are always with us."

We know that we cannot put the workings of God via His gift of holy spirit in a box. There are times when, either in private or in the congregation of saints worshiping of and praising God and magnifying His Word, phenomenal things can occur (See Appendix A). God can move in the exterior world in a way that seems to indicate that His presence comes and goes. A good biblical example of this is when the Temple was being consecrated in II Chronicles 5:14, and the glory of God filled the Temple so that the priests couldn't stand to minister.

That God moved in this way did not indicate His presence was with them on that occasion and not at other times. It shows that God is God and that He can reveal Himself and His power in a variety of ways. Those who experience phenomena must be careful to not build doctrine upon these experiences, as by assuming they are promised in God's Word or believing they indicate a special blessing on themselves or their ministries.

We also see a difference between the Old and New Testaments with regard to God's presence. In the Old Testament, it was considered something external, and there were places to go to be "in His presence" (the Tabernacle, the Temple, the burning bush, etc.). In the New Testament, God is in Christ (II Corinthians 5:21, et al), and He is the "place" to go to be in the presence of God. When a person accepts Jesus Christ as his Lord and Savior, God's Word teaches that the presence of God in Christ comes into the believer (John 17:23;14:23). Jesus Christ promised to be continually with us (Matthew 28:20), which promise was brought to pass with the giving of the gift of holy spirit on the day of Pentecost.

Receiving and Releasing

Two words that need to be properly understood in the context of the gift of holy spirit are the Greek words *dechomai* and *lambano*. The Greek word *lambano* has a wide range of meanings in the New Testament, and some of the ways it is translated in the King James Version include "receive" (133), "attain" (1), "bring" (1), "call to" (1), "hold" (1), "take away" (1), "take to one's self" (1), "take upon one's self" (1), "accept" (2), "obtain" (2), "take up" (2), "catch" (3), "have" (3), and "take" (104).

Lambano also has an overlap of meanings with other Greek words, particularly *dechomai*. *Lambano,* however, has an emphasis on the *action* taken by the one receiving. *Vine's Dictionary Of New Testament Words* notes: "There is a distinction between *lambano* and *dechomai* (more pronounced in the earlier, classical use), in that in many instances *lambano* suggests a self-prompted taking, whereas *dechomai* more frequently indicates "a welcoming or an appropriating reception" [38]

"Self-prompted taking" is a key phrase. Too many Christans wait for God to move them instead of reaching out and taking hold of what God has already given them. *The New Thayer's Greek-English Lexicon* adds, "...the suggestion of self-prompted taking still adheres to [*lambano*] in many connections ...in distinction from [*dechomai* being] a receiving of what is offered." [39]

The word *lambano* is used 263 times in the Greek New Testament and it is the exclusive word translated "receive" in relation to the gift of holy spirit. Consider the following verses in which the word "receive" is *lambano*.

John 20:22

And with that he breathed on them and said, "Receive the Holy Spirit [no article—read "holy spirit"]."

---

38. W.E. Vine, *The Expanded Vines Expository Dictionary of Net Testament Words* (Bethany House Publishers, Minneapolis MN, 1984), "Receive", page 928.

---

39. *The New Thayer's Greek-English Lexicon*, page 31.

Acts 1:8

But you will receive power when the Holy Spirit [holy spirit] comes on you; and you will be my witnesses in Jerusalem, and in all Judea and Samaria, and to the ends of the earth."

Acts 2:33

Exalted to the right hand of God, he has received from the Father the promised Holy Spirit [read "holy spirit"] and has poured out what you now see and hear.

Acts 2:38

Peter replied, "Repent and be baptized, every one of you, in the name of Jesus Christ for the forgiveness of sins. And you will receive the gift of the Holy Spirit [no article— read "holy spirit"].

Romans 8:15

For you did not receive a spirit that makes you a slave again to fear, but you received the Spirit [no article—read "a spirit"] of sonship. And by him we cry, "Abba, Father."

Galatians 3:2

I would like to learn just one thing from you: Did you receive the Spirit [spirit] by observing the law, or by believing what you heard?

In every one of the above verses, the word "receive" is a translation of the Greek word *lambano*. Studying these uses of *lambano* in connection with the gift of holy spirit shows us that when someone "receives" or "takes" the holy spirit, there is a visible and tangible manifestation (evidence) to others present.

In Acts, Chapter Eight, under the ministry of Philip, many people in the city of Samaria were saved. It is quite clear from the context that the people of Samaria had been saved, because Acts 8:14 says they "had accepted the Word of God." Note that in this verse the word "accepted" is *dechomai*. The people of Samaria had welcomed the Word of the Lord, but there was still a "self-prompted taking" that had not occurred. The people were saved, but they had missed *doing* something, that is, receiving the gift into manifestation, exhibiting it. Peter and John came to Samaria, and the people "received" [*lambano*] the holy spirit. When the people "received" [*lambano*] the holy spirit, there was tangible proof, for Simon the sorcerer "saw" evidence that the spirit was given.

Acts 8:14-17

When the apostles in Jerusalem heard that Samaria had accepted [*dechomai*] the word of God, they sent Peter and John to them.

When they arrived, they prayed for them that they might receive [*lambano*] the Holy Spirit [no article—read "holy spirit"],because the Holy Spirit [the text reads "it"] had not yet come upon any of them; they had simply been baptized into the name of the Lord Jesus. [40]

Then Peter and John placed their hands on them, and they received [*lambano*] the Holy Spirit [no article—read "holy spirit"].

---

40. Three pertinent verses to be properly understood with regard to the gift of holy spirit are Acts 8:16; 10:44 and 11:15. Most versions translate these verses to say that holy spirit "falls" on people, which makes it seem as though holy spirit came upon them and acted upon them without their consent. For example, the *KJV* of Acts 8:16 and 17 reads "(For as yet he was fallen upon [the Greek word for "fallen upon" is *epipipto*] none of them: only they were baptized in the name of the Lord Jesus. Then laid they their hands on them, and they received the Holy Ghost").

While it is true that the word *epipipto* can be understood as someone or something falling on someone, it does not have to be understood that way. Another usage of *epipipto* is when something "falls upon," i.e., happens to, or occurs in the life of someone. For example, Luke 1:12 describes what happened to Zechariah when he saw the angel in the Temple. The *KJV* says that fear "fell" on him. Fear did not fall on him as if it were coming from the sky. Fear was Zechariah's own response when he unexpectedly saw the angel. Another example is Romans 15:3, which says "For even Christ did not please himself, but, as it is written: 'The insults of those who insult you have fallen on me.'" The insults in this verse did not "fall" on Christ, as if they came from the sky, but rather they happened to Him, or occurred in his life.

Such examples help us properly understand the three difficult verses in Acts that are listed above. A careful study of these verses indicates that holy spirit did not "fall" from the sky upon the disciples, but that they experienced in manifestation the gift of holy spirit already within them.

The context of Acts, Chapter Eight makes this very clear. The disciples in Samaria were indeed born again, but had never manifested holy spirit outwardly by speaking in tongues, interpretation, prophecy, etc. Acts 8:16 indicates that those believers had not had the holy spirit "fall," i.e., "happen" or "occur" to them, but when Peter and John laid hands on them (verse 17), they all received into evidence *(lambano)* holy spirit they had already received internally (*dechomai*—verse 14).

Similarly, in Acts Chapter Ten, Peter had tangible proof of the intangible presence of holy spirit that was inside the Gentile believers. In Acts 10:46, they were speaking in tongues, to which Peter responded, "Can anyone keep these people from being baptized with water? They have received [*lambano*] the Holy Spirit [holy spirit] just as we have" (Acts 10:47). Had he not seen tangible proof of holy spirit within them, Peter would have been very skeptical as to whether or not *Gentiles* could have really been saved in the same manner as the Jews. He saw that proof when the new converts spoke in tongues, which is listed in I Corinthians 12 as a manifestation (evidence) of the spirit. It is significant that the text says that the Gentiles "received [*lambano*] holy spirit."

Another clear case linking the word *lambano* to a "receiving" that is tangible is in Acts 19. On his travels, the Apostle Paul came to Ephesus.

Acts 19:1,2

While Apollos was at Corinth, Paul took the road through the interior and arrived at Ephesus. There he found some disciples and asked them, "Did you receive the Holy Spirit [no article—read "holy spirit"] when you believed?" They answered, "No, we have not even heard that there is a Holy Spirit [holy spirit]." [41]

Here again it is clear that Paul was looking for some external and tangible proof of holy spirit dwelling within those disciples. Allow us to give a contemporary-youth rendition of Acts 19:2-5.

Paul said, "How 'bout that holy spirit?"

They said, "Huh?"

Paul asked them, "What d'ya mean 'Huh?' If you weren't baptized in holy spirit, what were you baptized in?"

---

41. Both the definite article "the" and the indefinite article "a" preceding the words "holy spirit" in the above two verses were placed in the English by the translators, despite their absence in the Greek text. Although the indefinite article can be supplied since the Greek language does not have one, the definite article cannot be. Neither is in the text, and verse two should be translated as follows, "Did you receive holy spirit when you believed?" They answered, "No, we have not even heard that there is holy spirit." All that these disciples had heard about was John the Baptist's water baptism, which preceded, and had been superseded by, holy spirit baptism.

They replied, "John's baptism—water, bro."

Paul then said, "John's baptism was right on, but check this out—the Messiah guy John's baptism pointed to has come, and He's got a new baptism thing."

They said, "Like, that's cool—let's go for it."

How did they, and Paul, then *know* they were born again and filled with holy spirit? Because they *manifested* the spirit they had just received by speaking in tongues and prophesying (verse 6).

In our concluding section, we will see that God has graciously given each Christian a guarantee of the divine deposit that the Lord Jesus put within him. Infallible proof of the veracity of God's Word, of the resurrection of Jesus Christ and of the assurance of everlasting life in Paradise is available to every Christian.

A Guaranteed Saving Deposit

Most people are very concerned about their futures. In fact, they would pay dearly for information about what is going to happen to them in the days to come. The 1-900 Psychic Hotline is jammed with calls by people seeking to hear about their futures from someone supposedly tapped into the mind of the universe (or who at least reads *The National Enquirer*).

With one's concern for the future comes a corresponding concern for his security. He may open a savings account that he is told is "guaranteed" by the government. After a good belly laugh, he begins making savings deposits that he hopes will accrue to his future wellbeing. In this final section, we will set forth a great truth—one of the most important reasons why you as a Christian must know that you have been given the precious gift of holy spirit. As we will see, it is your guaranteed *saving* deposit.

Let us begin by looking at a stupendous section of Scripture that shows how each Christian has come from death unto life via God's grace. Note the liquid terminology in regard to the new birth and the gift of holy spirit "poured out" upon each of us.

Titus 3:3-8 (*Amplified Version*)

For we also were once thoughtless *and* senseless, obstinate *and* disobedient, deluded *and* misled; [we too were once] slaves to all sorts of cravings *and* pleasures, wasting our days in malice and jealousy *and* envy, hateful (hated, detestable) and hating one another.

But when the goodness and loving kindness of God our Savior to man...appeared,

He saved us, not because of any works of righteousness that we had done, but because of His own pity *and* mercy, by [the] cleansing (bath) of the new birth (regeneration and renewing of the holy spirit,

Which He poured oùt [so] richly upon us through Jesus Christ our Savior.

[And He did it in order] that we might be justified by His grace— by His favor, wholly undeserved, that is, that we might be acknowledged and counted as conformed to the Divine will in purpose, thought and action; and that we might become heirs of eternal life according to [our] hope.

This message is most trustworthy, and concerning these things I want you to insist steadfastly, so that those who have believed in (trusted, relied on) God may be careful to apply themselves to honorable occupations *and* to doing good, for such things are [not only] excellent *and* right [in themselves], but [they are] good *and* profitable for the people.

To know beyond any shadow of a doubt that you are saved from death unto everlasting life in Paradise should bring indescribable joy and peace to your heart each day, and should be the firm foundation upon which you stand amidst the trials and tribulations of this present evil age. Such knowledge is a lot more reassuring than anything you'll hear from the Psychic Hotline. But what infallible *proof* of our future destiny do we have? What guarantee of our salvation is there? As always, God has the answer, and we can take His Word for it. So let's do, by again looking at some verses previously discussed in Chapter Two.

II Corinthians 1:18-22

But as surely as God is faithful, our message to you is not "Yes" and "No."

For the Son of God, Jesus Christ, who was preached among you by me and Silas and Timothy, was not "Yes" and "No," but in him it has always been "Yes."

For no matter how many promises God has made, they are "Yes" in Christ. And so through him the "Amen" is spoken by us to the glory of God.

Now it is God who makes both us and you stand firm in Christ. He anointed us, set his seal of ownership on us, and put his Spirit [spirit] in our hearts as a deposit, guaranteeing what is to come.

Go ahead and quiver with delight—we'll wait. Look at those glorious words! For our purposes in this book, the last two verses are especially electrifying. In verses 21 and 22, we see that every Christian is anointed, sealed and owned by God. In verse 22, the word "deposit" is the Greek word *arrabon*, and is its first of only three uses in God's Word. It means a pledge, a downpayment or a deposit. In the *King James Version*, it is translated as "earnest," as in "earnest money" given by one person to another to solidify a transaction.

The Lord Jesus Christ has given us the gift of holy spirit as a pledge, a downpayment or a deposit. This gift is now contained in our corrupted physical bodies that will eventually die, and therefore it is not "everlasting life" *per se*. It is, however, our absolute *guarantee* that one day, at His appearing, He will "pay off in full," that is, He will change our bodies to be like His own. At that time, we will have brand new bodies and live "happily ever after" on a new earth with the Lord and all believers. The following verses contain the second use of *arrabon* ("deposit") and illustrate the truth that holy spirit is our guarantee of a new body and everlasting life:

II Corinthians 5:1-5

Now we know that if the earthly tent we live in is destroyed, we have a building from God, an eternal house in heaven, not built by human hands.

Meanwhile we groan, longing to be clothed with our heavenly dwelling, because when we are clothed, we will not be found naked.

For while we are in this tent, we groan and are burdened, because we do not wish to be unclothed, but to be clothed with our heavenly dwelling, so that what is mortal may be swallowed up by life.

Now it is God who has made us for this very purpose and has GIVEN US THE SPIRIT [spirit] AS A DEPOSIT, GUARANTEEING WHAT IS TO COME.

The third and final use of *arrabon* is equally edifying:

Ephesians 1:13, 14 (*Amplified Version*)

In Him you also who have heard the Word of Truth, the glad tidings (Gospel) of your salvation, and have believed in *and* have adhered to *and* have relied on Him, were stamped with the seal of the long-promised Holy Spirit [holy spirit].

That Spirit [spirit] is the guarantee of our inheritance—the first fruit, the pledge and foretaste, the downpayment [*arrabon*] on our heritage— in anticipation of its full redemption *and* our acquiring [complete] possession of it, to the praise of His glory.

The gift of holy spirit is our guarantee of life in the age to come, as well as our guarantee that all the other promises in God's Word are true, and that we can by faith appropriate them *today*. However, a logical question must be asked: How can you as a Christian *know* that holy spirit is within you, since you cannot feel it. Some would answer that you can know because God promised to give it to you, and we would say "Amen." But in His grace and love, and because of how well He understands our human frailty, God has given us an indisputable sign, an "infallible proof" in the senses realm that Jesus Christ is alive and that He lives within us via holy spirit. [42]

God knows that you cannot feel His holy spirit within you. He also knows that at times every Christian fails to obey Him, and that therefore there can be no *behavioral* standard for whether or not someone is really "saved." The world is full of "nice" people who have no relationship with Christ, and with Christians who aren't acting like Christians. God's Word tells us that the intangible holy spirit within us is our guarantee of life in the age to come. It also tells

---

42. This is a truth that is elaborated upon in great detail in our audio-tape seminar, *Introduction To God's Heart.*

us there is a tangible manifestation of the spirit that proves its residence within us, and that manifestation is *speaking in tongues.*

It is most significant that seven of the nine manifestations listed in I Corinthians 12:8-10 were in operation before Pentecost. Only speaking in tongues and interpretation of tongues are unique to the "Church age" that began on Pentecost. Why? Because when the new birth of incorruptible seed became available, the corresponding proof of speaking in tongues (and its companion manifestation of interpretation of tongues) was necessitated.

A study of the Book of Acts shows that the pattern in the early church was that when a person believed on Jesus Christ as Lord, he was taught about speaking in tongues and he immediately did so. The same thing should be happening today, and where the Word of God is taught accurately in regard to this truth, it is. Speaking in tongues is the "witness" to you of holy spirit within you. We have seldom seen the following verses taught in this light, but we believe that the witness of holy spirit within each believer is exactly what they are all about:

I John 5:5-13 (*KJV*)

Who is he that overcometh the world, but he that believeth that Jesus is the Son of God?

This is He That came by water and blood, *even* Jesus Christ; not by water only, but by water and blood. And it is the spirit that beareth witness, because the Spirit [spirit] is truth.

For there are three that bear record [witness]...[texts omit 7b and 8a]...

The Spirit [spirit], and the water, and the blood: and these three agree in one.

If we receive the witness of men, the witness of God is greater: for this is the witness of God which He hath testified [witnessed] of His Son.

He that believeth on the Son of God hath the witness in himself: he that believeth not God hath made Him a liar; because he believeth not the record [witness] that God gave of His Son.

And this is the record [witness], [comma wrongly added] that God hath given to us eternal life [life in the age to come], and this life is in His Son.

He that hath the Son hath life; *and* he that hath not the Son of God hath not life.

These things have I written unto you... [texts omit the *KJV* words we have omitted here] that ye may know that ye have eternal life [life in the age to come], and that ye may believe on the name of the Son of God.

Verse 5 says that Jesus is the Son of God. Verse 6 is referring to His physical birth, which involved water and blood, like all human births. Verse 6 says also that holy spirit in us is our witness that Jesus was born, died, was raised, has overcome the world and has made us overcomers also. We believe verses 7 and 8 are talking about the witness of the spirit in each believer ("in one"). This agrees with verse 10, which says that each believer has the witness "in himself."

Verse 11 is a gem, *if* you delete the man-added comma after the word "record" (witness). God is saying that the witness of the spirit in you (verse 10) is the witness that God has given you life in the age to come. Speaking in tongues makes you a *firsthand witness* of the resurrection of Jesus Christ. Hearsay won't stand up in a court of law, nor will it stand the test of Satan's accusations that you are maybe not even saved, and certainly not all that God says you are. When you speak in tongues, you have proof of the resurrected Christ that is just as "infallible" as the proof for those in Acts, Chapter One who saw and touched their risen Lord. God is no respecter of persons, praise His Name!

Understanding verses 5-12 as we have set forth brings verse 13 into focus, because otherwise the words in it look rather out of order. We know that it is by believing in Jesus Christ that one receives the life spoken of in verse 13. Then why does it say that those who know they have this guarantee of everlasting life need to "believe on the name of the Son of God"? The reason is that your absolute certainty of salvation is the foundation for your walk of faith, that is, believing and obeying the Lord Jesus Christ. Your proof that He has guaranteed you the salvation for which you trusted Him is also your proof that you can trust Him day by day in this life. The next two verses in I John 5 make that clear.

I John 5:14, 15 (*KJV*)

And this is the confidence that we have in Him, that if we ask anything according to His will, He heareth us:

And if we know that He hear us whatsoever we ask, we know that we have the petitions that we desired of Him.

Your future is as bright as the promises of God. You believed His promise of everlasting life, and, especially if you speak in tongues, you know *for sure* that your glorious future destiny will be fulfilled. Thus you can walk through this life with the same certainty about all the rest of God's promises, stepping out in obedience by faith, and expecting to see your heavenly Father fulfill his part of your fellowlaborer relationship. He will. AMEN!

Conclusion

The Habitation of God

We have seen that the gift of God, holy spirit, was given to produce fruitful work. The Greek words *energeo* and *energema*, both related to "work," indicate that the presence of holy spirit in us is not designed to titillate our emotions or conjure up experiences that we might desire, but rather "to profit" us and others as we manifest the spirit. We now want to view the gift of holy spirit from another perspective, that of God's desire to have a habitation in which to dwell among His people.

God is spirit (John 4:24), and is therefore invisible and intangible, but to those with holy spirit He can be known directly. To people without holy spirit, He can be known only as He reveals Himself in symbols or that which represents Him, whether it be words, inanimate objects (like an ark or a stone), prophets, angels or even jackasses that speak. God is awesome in glory and grandeur, and His creation speaks of His vastness, as Solomon exclaims in II Chronicles upon the occasion of the building of the Temple:

II Chronicles 6:18

"But will God really dwell on earth with men? The heavens, even the highest heavens, cannot contain you. How much less this temple I have built!"

This same thought is echoed in Isaiah:

Isaiah 57:15

For this is what the high and lofty One says—he who lives forever, whose name is holy: "I live in a high and holy place, but also with him who is contrite and lowly in spirit, to revive the spirit of the lowly and to revive the heart of the contrite.

Our vast and mighty God does not dwell in temples made with hands, as the Scripture declares in Paul's famous Athenian sermon:

Acts 17: 24,25

The God who made the world and everything in it is the Lord of heaven and earth and does not live in temples built by hands.

And he is not served by human hands, as if he needed anything, because he himself gives all men life and breath and everything else.

In Stephen's address to the Sanhedrin, this same truth is boldly proclaimed:

Acts 7: 44-50

Our fathers had the tabernacle of the Testimony with them in the desert. It had been made as God directed Moses, according to the pattern he had seen.

Having received the tabernacle, our fathers under Joshua brought it with them when they took the land from the nations God drove out before them. It remained in the land until the time of David,who enjoyed God's favor and asked that he might provide a dwelling place for the God of Jacob.

But it was Solomon who built the house for him.

However, the Most High does not live in houses made by men. As the prophet says:

Heaven is my throne, and the earth is my footstool. What kind of house will you build for me? says the Lord. Or where will my resting place be?

Has not my hand made all these things?

Israel's early sanctuaries for the worship of the One True God were set up in the places where He appeared to His people or "caused his name to dwell." The sanctuary was a place people could go to be in His presence. It represented the coming Messiah and His mediation and sacrifice for the sins of Israel, and ultimately all mankind (see Hebrews 9:9-14). Both the Tabernacle and the Temple were physical symbols of the spiritual truth that God was to be in Christ, reconciling the world unto himself.

In Exodus 25:8, God commands Moses to speak to the children of Israel and have those who were willing give materials to build a "sanctuary" where God would (symbolically) dwell with them.

Exodus 25:9

Make this tabernacle and all its furnishings exactly like the pattern, I will show you.

God gave Moses a detailed "blueprint" for the building and furnishing of a tabernacle, or sanctuary, in which He would dwell in a visible way among them. Moses, however, did not build the building. Instead, Bezaleel, Aholiab and wise-hearted men (Exodus 31:1-6) built it as God enabled and equipped them to perform this monumental task.

Exodus 31:3

And I have filled him with the Spirit of God, with skill, ability and knowledge in all kinds of crafts—

Note that it was the spirit of God upon these men that equipped them to do the work. We see the same principles in the record of the building of the Temple, a more permanent place of worship, and the place where God would dwell among the children of Israel. David had it in his heart to build a house for the Lord, but God gave the pattern for the Temple to him, as the pattern for the Tabernacle had been given to Moses:

I Chronicles 28:11,12

Then David gave his son Solomon the plans for the portico of the temple, its buildings, its storerooms, its upper parts, its inner rooms and the place of atonement.

He gave him the plans of all that the Spirit had put in his mind for the courts of the temple of the Lord and all the surrounding rooms, for the treasuries of the temple of God and for the treasuries for the dedicated things.

But because David was a man of war (I Chronicles 28:3), he did not build it himself. God gave him a son, Solomon, who built it instead (I Chronicles 22:19). Solomon did not actually build it himself, but further delegated the building to Huram Abi, a man of Tyre (II Chronicles 2:13). Surely we can assume that his understanding also came from the spirit of God upon him, as it was with Bezaleel and Aholiab.

The Tabernacle and the Temple were the best God could do, so to speak, to be with all His people until His Son Jesus Christ lived, died, was raised from the dead and exalted as Lord. On the day of Pentecost, when Jesus Christ first poured out the gift of holy spirit into people's hearts, the building of a new Temple began, giving all people equal access to God. The epistle to the Ephesians expresses some profound truths about this dwellingplace of God

Ephesians 2:19-22

Consequently, you are no longer foreigners and aliens, but fellow citizens with God's people and members of God's household, built on the foundation of the apostles and prophets, with Christ Jesus himself as the chief cornerstone. In him the whole building is joined together and rises to become a holy temple in the Lord. And in him you too are being built together to become a dwelling in which God lives by his Spirit.

Note the architectural metaphor referring to Jesus Christ as the "chief cornerstone." Ancient buildings were built by the laying of stone blocks. The first block set in the first corner was the most important one of all, for it established every angle and line of the entire building. It also set the level for the foundation and the squareness of the walls. Built upon the cornerstone of this spiritual Temple are the apostles and prophets who are the foundation. The saints, both Jew and Gentile, are the walls and the roof of the building, which is a spiritual dwellingplace for God. The means by which this Temple is being built is holy spirit, enabling the saints to do the work of the ministry.

God's Word makes plain the truth that He does not dwell in physical buildings. Because God was in Christ, reconciling the world to Himself (II Corinthians 5:21), Christ, then, is the "place" to go to be in God's presence. When a person believes in Christ, he becomes a new creation, God's workmanship ("masterpiece"— Ephesians 2:10). God dwells in the believer as He dwelled in Christ, and His presence is within the believer via the precious gift of holy spirit. This gift makes every believer a sanctuary, a place of worship, a place to be in God's presence.

Also, every believer is connected to every other believer by holy spirit (i.e., the "unity of the spirit"— Ephesians 4:3) as each is a part of the building of the invisible Temple. Jesus Christ is overseeing this building, which is the Church, His "body" (Ephesians 1:23). As Moses and David received the patterns for the building of temporal dwellingplaces for God, so Jesus Christ has been given the pattern for a spiritual Temple. Jesus Christ is not building this "Temple" alone, but has delegated much of the responsibility for it

to us, the believers. We do the building according to His specifica-
tions, as it was revealed to Him. To us is committed the word
and the ministry of reconciliation (II Corinthians 5:18,19). What a
privilege to share with our Lord Jesus the building of God's eternal
household. We are fellowlaborers with Him, as we manifest the
gift of holy spirit together with our brothers and sisters in the family
of God.

Shortly before His death, Jesus told his disciples that He would
send them "another" Comforter, or Counselor. He was referring to
holy spirit, which would take His place with them. In fact, Jesus
said it would be *in* them. Think of the implications of this truth. Via
the spirit of God within you, it is possible for you to have a
relationship with Jesus Christ similar to how it would be if He were
physically present with you moment by moment. That should
brighten your day—and your life!

Completely Completely Complete

We believe that the Body of Christ can benefit from the biblical
truths set forth in this simple book. Think of the confusion and
division that can be eliminated. Think of the "ego trips" that will
evaporate, and of the defeated Christians who will walk in the
victory Jesus Christ has won for them.

Praise God for His faithfulness to His Word, and for His
magnanimity to all who call upon Him. How infinitely wise of Him
to give each believer the same spiritual gift, His own divine nature,
and then help each one of us utilize the gift in ways that best enable
each of us to be individually fulfilled, while simultaneously fulfilling God's overall purposes for the Church.

As a Christian, you are completely, completely *complete* in
Christ (Colossians 2:10). You lack nothing. You have been *blessed*
with all spiritual blessings (Ephesians 1:3). You have obtained the
guarantee of an *inheritance* (Ephesians 1:14). You are *filled* with all
the fulness of God (Ephesians 3:19). You are *sealed* unto the day of
redemption (Ephesians 4:30).

What do all these magnificent truths mean to you today? They mean that you can experientially know Jesus Christ and the power of His resurrection (Philippians 3:10). You can let the Word of Christ dwell in you richly in all wisdom (Colossians 3:16). As God's masterpiece, you can do the good works to which He has called you (Ephesians 2:10). You can walk worthy of the calling of God (Ephesians 4:1), no matter what the circumstances in your life are like.

In his translation of the New Testament titled *The Message*, Eugene Peterson writes in his "Introduction to Philippians" about Paul having written this joyous epistle while in prison:

> But circumstances are incidental compared to the life of Jesus, the Messiah, that Paul experiences from the inside. For it is a life that not only happened at a certain point in history, but continues to happen, spilling out into the lives of those who receive him, and then continues to spill out all over the place. Christ is, among much else, the revelation that God cannot be contained or hoarded. It is the "spilling out" quality of Christ's life that accounts for the happiness of Christians, for joy is life in excess, the overflow of what cannot be contained within any one person.

You have been baptized, anointed and filled with the life-giving nature, power and love of God Almighty, the Creator of the heavens and the earth. Because you have drunk from the rivers of living water, you have within you "a bubbling fountain" that will never dry up. Each moment of each day you can draw from this fathomless well within you, and then pour out your heart and your life to those around you who thirst as you did. You can do so knowing that you will never run dry, and that because of the precious gift of holy spirit, you always have whatever resources you need to do whatever God asks you to do. Praise His holy Name!

What About Phenomena?

I n this book, we talked about discerning a spiritual counterfeit from a godly spiritual experience. We also discussed the reciprocal relationship between God and His people, but there are occasions when God goes "above and beyond" this reciprocal relationship. That is, He acts independently of our cooperation, and does what can be called "phenomena." Phenomena are supernatural manifestations of the power of God as He acts in the physical universe in ways that are creative, responsive to particular situations and often unpredictable. As such, they will never be at odds with His written Word, and will, in fact, significantly support what He has revealed about His character and His methods.

Phenomena are not the action of the gift of holy spirit within a believer, because this requires the person's cooperation. Phenomena are not visions or subjective experiences. They are not promised to God's people, nor can they be expected or demanded. They happen because God chooses to manifest His power in some particular way for His own purposes and glory, and they can be perceived by unbelievers, whether or not they understand what is going on.

Phenomena display God's creativity and awesome power as the Creator and Sustainer of the universe— "that all may know that I am the Lord your God" (Exodus 6:7). Though we cannot totally comprehend the whole of His purposes in manifesting phenomena, we can discern that at various times phenomena show forth His judgment, mercy, protection, glory and approval.

Some examples of phenomena are: the flood of Noah; the scattering of languages at the tower of Babel; fire and brimstone raining upon Sodom and Gomorrah; the pillar of fire at night and the cloud by day that led Israel through the wilderness; the finger of God writing the law onto tablets of stone; fire falling from heaven to light the sacrifices; the earth swallowing up Dothan; Balaam's donkey talking to him; the writing that appeared on the wall at Beltshazzar's feast; Zachariah's muteness; the darkness upon the earth the afternoon of Christ's crucifixion; the earthquake that rolled back the stone on His sepulchre; the cloven tongues of fire and sound of the mighty wind on Pentecost; the house shaking (Acts 4); the brilliant light and Paul's subsequent blindness; the Philippian prison earth-quake; the appearance of angels throughout the Word; and perhaps the ultimate phenomenon that is still to come— the melting of the present heavens and earth with fervent heat.

What can we then say to these things, except that God will be God and move upon the earth in "ways that are not our ways" (Isaiah 55:8). The power and variety of these biblically-recorded phenomena lead us to be cautious as we evaluate current so-called phenomena that the Bible does not specifically sanction, for we have seen that God is infinitely creative and often unpredictable. It is clear, though, that each of these phenomena had a purpose and a profit, which in some cases was simply to mark out some event as being of God. Who but our God can make the heavens shake and man to bow before Him in abject reverence? Yet, we want to emphasize once again that God's ways will be in concert with His character of love and justice as revealed in His written Word.

In regard to this issue, we must distinguish between the genuine power of God in action and the emotional or physical reaction that a person may have in response to it. His power is awesome and ultimate, and in His righteous and holy presence, the sinful man of flesh may "crumble" (II Chronicles 5:14), "faint" (Daniel 10:8), "quake" (Daniel 10:7), "shake" (Matthew 28:4), "tremble" (Daniel 10:11), "be unable to stand" (II Chronicles 5:14), "become as a dead man" (Matthew 28:4), "be hindered" (II Chronicles 7:2), "become blind for a season" (Acts 9:8), "become dumb" (Luke 1:20), "fall to the ground" (Acts 9:4), "become as one whom wine has overcome" (Jeremiah 23:9), "fall on his knees" (II Kings 1:13), "fall on his face" (Genesis 17:3).

Therefore, let us not put God in any box of our own making, and let us beseech Him to continue to expand our understanding of His glory and power, and to grant us discernment to perceive the counterfeit spirit power manifested by His archenemy, the Devil. God's power will be manifest among those who seek to glorify, honor and serve Him, the only true God, and His wonderful Son Jesus Christ.

Appendix

B

The Flexible Usage of "God" and "Lord"

I t is very strange to most modern English speakers to think of anyone called "God" except God the Father of the Lord Jesus Christ. This is just not the case in the Greek and Hebrew languages in which the Bible was written. Just as in English the word "president" has flexibility and can refer to persons other than the President of the United States, so in the ancient Greek and Hebrew the word "GOD" (or "god", because the most ancient manuscripts were written in all capital or all lowercase letters) can refer to a number of different beings.

The *Theological Wordbook Of The Old Testament* (R. Laird Harris, editor, Moody Press, Chicago, 1980, Vol 1, under # 93, *el, eloah*) lists the meanings of *elohim* as "God, gods, judges, angels." A study of the uses of *elohim* will show it being used many times of both the true God and of idol gods. It is also used of spirit beings (see I Samuel 28:13; Genesis 32:30 [Jacob actually wrestled with an angel, who was God's representative, as Hosea 12:4 says]). It is also used of rulers and judges because they represent God on earth (Exodus 22:8,9,28; Psalm 82:1,6). This point would be easily understood by the Jews of biblical times, who knew that when someone sent an agent, it was as if the principal himself were present. The *Encyclopedia Of The Jewish Religion* notes that "the main point of the Jewish law of agency is expressed in the dictum, 'a person's agent is regarded as the person himself'" (R.J.Z. Werblowsky and G. Wigoder, editors, Adama Books, New York, 1986, page 15, "Agent"). In Psalm 45:6, "*Elohim*" is also used prophetically of Jesus Christ as Messiah.

Similarly, the *Theological Wordbook* lists the uses of *el* as "God, god, mighty one, strength." As with *elohim*, different uses can be clearly seen by using a concordance. Psalm 82:1 uses *el* in the first line, which could be translated as "God stands in the assembly of the mighty" ["the mighty" is "*el*"], where *el* is used of human rulers, just as *elohim* is used in the last half of the first verse. Another excellent example is Ezekiel 31:11, where *el* is translated "ruler," and in this particular prophecy refers to the king of Babylon.

Once one understands the flexible usage of "God" in both Hebrew and Greek, the reference to God's Messiah as "God" is not troublesome at all, and fits exactly with earthly rulers and judges (and spirit beings) being called "God."

Just as *elohim* and ("God") have a wide range of meanings, so does the word *kurios,* or "lord," as per all the lexicons we checked. The list that *The Complete Word Study New Testament* (Spiros Zodhiates, ed. AMG Publishers, Chattanooga TN, 1992, page 900, 901), gave was typical: Lord, master, owner." It then went on to list a number of different categories. Among them were: "the possessor, owner, master, e.g., of property" (Matthew 20:8) [in this verse the *NIV* actually translates "lord" as "owner"]; "master or head of a house" (Mark 13:35) [again the *NIV* translates "lord" as "owner" here]; "master of people, servants or slaves (Matthew 10:24; 24:45, 46, 48, 50; Acts 16:16). In these verses the word "lord," *kurios,* is translated "master" or "owner" by the *NIV.*

Kurios ("lord") is used of a husband in I Peter 3:6. It is used when someone has complete authority over something, as in "lord of the harvest" (Matthew 9:38). It is used of political rulers, as in Acts 25:26 where the Roman emperor was called "lord" (which is translated as "His Majesty" in the *NIV*). It is used of the pagan gods, as is clear from I Corinthians 8:5. It is also used of God the Father, and it is used of the Lord Jesus Christ. The point should be clear. We today may have a very limited use of the words "God" and "lord," but the writers of the Bible did not. We must be true to the definitions of these (and other) words as they are actually used in the Word of God, rather than import our theology back into the text of the Bible and make it say something other than what God intended.

Appendix

C

Usages Of "Spirit" In The New Testament

In any language, most words have at least two usages, and some have quite a number. This is the case with *pneuma,* which in the New Testament is most often translated as "spirit." In 1905, in his book *The Giver And His Gifts,* Dr. E.W. Bullinger wrote about the different ways in which *pneuma* is used:

The Use of *Pneuma* in the New Testament

Let us next note the various ways in which the Greek word *pneuma,* is employed: i.e., the way in which it is used (apart from its meanings, or the sense which is given to it: i.e., its usage):

    i. It is used alone, in two ways

1. without the article: simply *pneuma*

2. with the article: the *pneuma*

    ii. It is employed with *hagion* ("holy") in four ways:

1. *pneuma hagion* (holy spirit) Matt. 1:18, and in 49 other places.

2. *hagion pneuma* (spirit holy) I Cor. 6:19, etc.

3. the *hagion pneuma,* Matt. 28:19, etc.

4. the *pneuma* the *hagion,* Matt. 12:32, etc.

    iii. It is used with *pronouns*: e.g., the *pneuma* of me: i.e., my *pneuma,* Matt 12:18, etc.

    iv. It is used with *prepositions,* which affect its sense:

1. (*en pneumati*), by or through the Spirit: denoting agency.

2. Adverbially, as meaning spiritually and sometimes (like *en dolo*), craftily, II Cor. 12:16): thus turning the phrase into an *adverb.*

    v. It is employed in combination with the Divine Names in seven different forms; of which four have the article, and three are without: e.g., *pneuma Theou; pneuma Christou*, etc.

vi. It is employed with ten other nouns in the genitive case, which (by *Enallage*) qualify the meaning of *pneuma.* These again are used with and without the article: e.g., a *pneuma* of sonship (Rom. 8:15), i.e., a sonship *pneuma.*

vii. It is employed with a second noun with which it is joined by a conjunction (*Hendiadys*). Thus used it becomes a superlative adjective.

Here are seven different ways in which the word *pneuma* is employed. Each class is distinct, to say nothing of the minor variations.

Now, the question is, are we to make no difference in our reading and understanding of these various uses? Can it be that God employs the word *pneuma* in all these different ways, and yet has no object in so doing and has only one meaning for them all?

Surely, no one will contend that this is the case. [43]

A comparison of three English versions of the Bible, readily available at bookstores today, shows the different ways that translators have translated *pneuma:*

	KJV	*NIV*	*ASV*
Spirit	137	241	239
spirit or spirits	151	116	135
Spirit's	0	2	0
Ghost	89	0	0
ghost	2	2	0
life	1	0	0
wind	1	1	1
winds	0	1	1
breath	0	3	3

---

43. Bullinger, *The Giver And His Gift,* page 11-12.

	KJV	*NIV*	*ASV*
spiritually	1	0	0
spiritual	1	2	1
attitude	0	1	0
demon-possessed	0	1	0
heart	0	1	0
mind	0	1	0
prophecy	0	1	0

Note: Not included on this list are other uses of *pneuma* in combination with other words, as this is meant to be only an indicator of some of the different ways *pneuma* has been translated.

The above table shows that translators chose to translate *pneuma* quite differently. The list that follows will show that even when the translators translated *pneuma* as "spirit," the reader must still be aware of the exact meaning, because "spirit" is used in a number of ways. The following list may not be exhaustive, but it does give an indication of the wide variety of usages that *pneuma* has.

1. *Pneuma* is used of an immaterial "substance." John 4:24 says, "God is spirit..."

2. *Pneuma* is used of God, the Creator of the universe and Father of the Lord Jesus Christ. Matthew 1:18 says that Mary was pregnant through "the Holy Spirit" [*pneuma*]. Many other verses clearly teach that Christ was the Son of God the Father, here called the "Holy Spirit" (because God is holy and God is spirit). In Acts 5:3, Peter told Ananias, "You have lied to the Holy Spirit," whom he identified in verse 4 as "God."

3. *Pneuma* is used of Jesus Christ, the Son of God, in His resurrected body. I Corinthians 15:45 says that Jesus Christ became a "life-giving spirit" [*pneuma*]. After his resurrection, Jesus is occasionally referred to as "the Spirit." "Now the Lord is the Spirit...the Lord, who is the Spirit" (II Corinthians 3:17,18). Christ is also referred to as "the Spirit" in Revelation 2:7,11,17,29; 3:6,13 and 22, as is clear from the con-

text.   Jesus is the one doing the talking.   Other noteworthy verses are Revelation 14:13 and 22:17.

4. *Pneuma* is used of the gift of God that was put upon certain believers before the day of Pentecost. Remember from the text of this book that before Pentecost, when God gave His gift of holy spirit to people, He: (a) gave it to only some people, (b) gave different measures to different people, and (c) could take it away from people, just as He did with King Saul and with Samson. As Scripture testifies, Jesus Christ had holy spirit put upon Him: "I will put my spirit [*pneuma*] on him" (Matthew 12:18). Holy spirit came upon Jesus at his baptism in Jordan, and instead of being only a measure of spirit like that upon so many in the Old Testament, Scripture states that Jesus was given "the spirit [*pneuma*] without measure" (John 3:34). Thus, in Luke 4:18, Jesus stated that "the spirit of the Lord is upon me..."   Some other New Testament believers who had holy spirit upon them before the day of Pentecost were Elizabeth (Luke 1:41), Zacharias (Luke 1:67) and Simeon (Luke 2:25).

5. *Pneuma* is used of God's gift, spirit (usually called "holy spirit") which has been given in birth (referred to as being "born again") to believers since the day of Pentecost. Peter was filled with holy spirit (Acts 4:8). Paul, amazed that the Galatian believers would try to go back to the law, wrote, "Did you receive the spirit [*pneuma*] by observing the law...?" (Galatians 3:2). When the Gentiles believed, they also received the gift of holy spirit (Acts 10:44,45). Ephesians calls this gift of holy spirit a "seal" that each believer receives at the time of his or her new birth (Ephesians 1:13). There were several prophecies given in the Gospels about the holy spirit to be given on the day of Pentecost. John 3:6 says "That which is born of Spirit [*pneuma*, God the Father] is spirit [*pneuma*, the gift of God, the spirit given via the new birth]." In John 7:38, Jesus spoke prophetically of this coming spirit, and verse 39 clearly says it was not given yet. Jesus spoke of a "spirit of truth" that had not yet come in His lifetime.

Even after His death and resurrection, Jesus told his disciples to "wait" for the spirit (Acts 1:5), and told them they would have power when it came (Acts 1:8), clearly indicating that its coming was still future. On the day of Pentecost, the apostles were all filled with holy spirit, and Peter told the multitude that the promised spirit was for them and their children as well as for the apostles (Acts 2:4,38,39). All of these uses refer to holy spirit, the promised gift of God that was given by Jesus Christ (Acts 2:33) to the apostles on the day of Pentecost and is now born inside each Christian.

6. *Pneuma* is used of angels, who are spirit beings. Hebrews 1:14 says, "Are not all angels ministering spirits [*pneumata*, the plural of *pneuma*]... See also Hebrews 1:7, where *pneumata* is translated "spirits" in most versions, and "winds" in the *NIV*.

7. *Pneuma* is used of evil or demon spirits many times in the Word of God. Matthew 10:1 says "He called his twelve disciples to him and gave them authority to drive out evil spirits [*pneumata*] and to heal every disease and sickness."

8. *Pneuma* is used of spirit beings that are not specifically delineated as either angels or evil spirits in the Word of God. Acts 23:9 says "some of the teachers of the law who were Pharisees stood up and argued vigorously. 'We find nothing wrong with this man,' they said. "What if a spirit [*pneuma*] or an angel has spoken to him?'" Revelation 1:4: 3:1; 4:5 and 5:6 are other examples of this.

9. *Pneuma* is used of the natural life of the body, which is more often described as the "soul" life, the *psuche*. As Christ was dying on the cross, He "gave up his spirit" [*pneuma*] (Matthew 27:50). What he gave up was His life, and the phrase used in Matthew—that he "gave up his spirit"—means that he died. A person did not die physically when holy spirit left, as examples from the Old Testament show. As it is used in Matthew 27:50, *pneuma* represents the life of the body. The same use of "spirit" is found in Luke 23:46,

when Christ said "Father, into your hands I commit my spirit." In Luke 8:55, Jesus raised a little girl from the dead, and the Bible says that "her spirit [*pneuma*] returned, and at once she stood up." Again, because holy spirit does not give the human body physical life, this use of *pneuma* refers to the natural life of her body. The same is true of James 2:26, which says that "the body without the spirit [*pneuma*, here referring to the "life"] is dead..."

10. *Pneuma* is used of the individual self or of the emotions, attitudes, thoughts, desires or will of a person. Although it might be possible to minutely divide these references, a broader viewpoint is appropriate for this study. Matthew 5:3 says, "Blessed are the poor in spirit [*pneuma*]..." Obviously, "poor in spirit" does not refer to the amount of holy spirit one has received from God, but rather refers to an attitude of meekness in the mind. Matthew 26:41 says, "The spirit [*pneuma*] is willing, but the body is weak." Here Christ was referring to the "spirit" as the operation of the mind, not the gift of holy spirit. Mark 8:12 (*KJV*) says, "And he sighed deeply in his spirit [*pneuma*], and saith, Why doth this generation seek after a sign?" Interestingly, the *NIV* translators picked up on the fact that holy spirit, the gift of God in Jesus, did not sigh, but rather it was an action of the mind, from the heart of Jesus' emotions, so they translated the verse "He sighed deeply [*pneuma*] and said..." "Sighed deeply" is exactly what Jesus did, represented in the Greek text as "sighed in his spirit."

II Corinthians 7:13 says, "...we were especially delighted to see how happy Titus was, because his spirit [*pneuma*] has been refreshed by all of you." The holy spirit born within a believer does not need refreshment. Thus, "spirit" here refers to his personal and emotional life, or possibly is used by the figure of speech *Synecdoche* for his entire self (see #11 below). Galatians 6:1 says, "Brothers, if someone is caught in a sin, you who are spiritual should restore him gently (literally "in a spirit [*pneuma*] of meekness). The *NIV* translators recognized that holy spirit was not being referred to, and used the phrase, "restore him gently," to refer to a humble attitude of mind.

11. *Pneuma* is used as a part of a person put in place of the whole person, via the figure of speech *Syne cdoche*. *The American Heritage Dictionary* defines *Synecdoche* as:

A figure of speech in which a part is used for the whole (as *hand* for *sailor*), the whole for a part (as *the law* for *police officer*), the specific for the general (as *cutthroat* for *assassin*), the general for the specific (as *thief* for *pickpocket*), or the material for the thing from which it is made (as *steel* for *sword*).

In *Figures Of Speech Used In The Bible*, (Baker Book House, Grand Rapids MI, reprinted 1968, pages 613-656), E.W. Bullinger gives many excellent examples of *Synecdoche* in the Bible. Under the category, "The Part For The Whole," Bullinger has 17 pages of examples. Among them are the following: "That no flesh [i.e., person] should glory in his presence" (I Corinthians 1:29); "Let us lay wait for blood [i.e., a person to kill]" (Proverbs 1:11); "Blessed are your eyes [i.e., you, not just your eyes]" (Matthew 13:16); "The froward mouth [i.e., froward speaking person] do I hate" (Proverbs 8:13); "Their feet [i.e., they] are swift to shed blood" (Romans 3:15; "Thy seed shall possess the gate [not just the gate, the whole city] of his enemies" (Genesis 22:17).

Similarly, there are clear examples where *pneuma* (spirit) is used for the whole person. In Luke 1:47, Mary says, "My spirit [not just her spirit, but her entire being] rejoices in God my Savior." In II Timothy 4:22, Paul wrote, "The Lord be with your spirit [obviously not just Timothy's spirit, but with Timothy as an entire person]." This same expression also occurs in Philemon, verse 6.

12. *Pneuma* is used by the figure of speech *Metonymy* for a related noun. *Metonymy* is defined in *The American Heritage Dictionary* as:

> A figure of speech in which one word or phrase is substituted for another with which it is closely associated, as in the use of *Washington* for the *United States government* or of the *sword* for *military power.*

> We use *Metonymy* in our speech when we say things such as "The White House said today... [i.e., a person in the White House"] or "Watch your mouth [i.e., be careful what you say]." Bullinger has 71 pages (pages 538-608) of examples of *Metonymy* in Scripture. A good example of *Metonymy* is found in John 6:63, when Christ said, "The words I have spoken to you are spirit..." Of course, the words themselves were not spirit, they were words, but they produced spiritual life in all those who believed.

The above categories are not exhaustive in their references, nor do the authors claim to have noted every distinction or even every category of usage of the word *pneuma*. The above list should, however, demonstrate that when one is reading the Bible, careful attention must be paid when the word "spirit" is used. A large amount of doctrinal error could quickly be corrected if Christians did not think of every use of "the Holy Spirit" as a reference to the third person of the "Trinity," but instead carefully read the context of the verse to see exactly what was meant by God, the Author. It would be much easier for the reader to do that if translators had not been so quick to add the article "the" before "holy spirit" where it does not belong, or to capitalize "spirit" almost everywhere it occurs. Even so, by careful reading the student of the Bible will usually be able to determine what God means when He uses the word "spirit."

Scripture

Index

A

Acts

Acts

C

I Chronicles

II Chronicles

Colossians

I Corinthians

II Corinthians

G

II Timothy

Titus

Topical

Index

relationship with God,
55-57
spirit-filled, 3-4
Church, 23
co-laborers with God, 55
Comforter, 20, 53
holy spirit as, 87
completeness in Christ, 88, 91
conduct of prophets, 58
control, 55-57
operating holy spirit, 58
cornerstone, Jesus Christ as,
86-87
Counselor, the, 87

D

David, 84-85
death, 11
as wages of sin, 12
dechomai, 70-75
demons, 103
casting out, 68
deposit, divine
holy spirit as, 7-8, 77-80
discerning of spirits, 68
divine nature, 14-15
donkey, Balaam's, 91
dorea, 65-66
Dothan, 91
dove, symbolism of, 37

E

Elijah, 25
spirit of, 52
Elisha, 25
Elizabeth, 44, 102
elohim, 95
Elymas the sorcerer, 44
Ephesus, 74

error, separating truth from,
39-40
Euroclydon, 59
evil spirits, 103

F

faith, 68-69
Father, as distinct from Son,
51
filled with the holy spirit,
40-43
filling into manifestation,
45
instances of, 43-45
translations of, 42-43
finger of God, 52
fire
pillar of, 91
tongues of, 22, 92
flood of Noah, 91
freedom of will, 60-61

G

Gentiles, salvation of, 74
gift of holy spirit
importance of distinction
from Giver, 53
nature of, 52-53
gifts
holy spirit, 65
versus manifestations, 62-
64
Giver, importance of distinction from gift, 53
God
as dance partner, 57-58
as Holy Spirit, 17-19, 51
believer's relationship with,
55-57

What Is Christian Educational Services?

C hristian Educational Services (CES) is a non-profit, tax exempt United States (Indiana) corporation whose purposes are to make known the Word of God, to further the gospel of the Lord Jesus Christ, to facilitate fellowship among Christians and to provide Christian educational services, including biblical research, written publications and biblical teachings. We do this via live speakers, tapes and literature. Our teachings point people to the Lordship of Jesus Christ in their lives. We encourage Christians to utilize these teachings in their local areas as they see fit.

The basis for all our efforts is the Bible, which we believe to be the Word of God, perfect in its original writing. So-called errors, contradictions or discrepancies are the result of man's subsequent interference in the transmission of the text, mistranslations or failure to understand what is written. CES draws from all relevant sources that shed light on the integrity of the Scriptures, whether in the field of geography, customs, language, history, or principles governing Bible interpretation. Our goal is to seek the truth without respect for tradition or "orthodoxy."

Any individual willing to examine his beliefs in the light of God's Word will perhaps profit from our teachings. They are non-denominational, and are intended to strengthen one's faith in God, Jesus Christ, and the Bible, no matter what his denominational preference may be. Designed primarily for individual home study, the teachings are the result of intensive research and rational methods, making them easy to follow, verify and practically apply. When accurately understood, the Word of God brings great deliverance from fear, doubt and worry, and leads the individual Christian to genuine freedom, confidence and joy in living. Beyond such practical blessings however, our goal is to enable the student to do biblical research for himself, so he is able to develop his own convictions, separate truth from error, and become an effective communicator of God's Word.

Biblical materials produced by CES are intended for each person's own use as he desires and as aids to local fellowships functioning independently as the Lord Jesus Christ directs them. Our goal is to serve people by educating them in Christian doctrine and practice. Biblical materials available from Christian Educational Services include:

Publications

Speaking The Truth In Love
The Purposes of Christian Educational Services

This book sets forth a brief overview of Church history from the Book of Acts until the present. It explores the historical development of Christian denominations and movements in light of three major issues that have either united or divided Christian people: church governance, church ceremony and church doctrine. Then it gives a general picture of what is available today in Christendom.

It goes on to define the purposes, mission, character and major doctrinal positions of Christian Educational Services. The uniqueness of what CES has to offer may be a desired alternative for many people who are sincerely seeking to know the truth of God's Word. The appendix gives a suggested biblical model for local church governance. COST: $4 (includes postage).

Is There Death After Life?

This book gives biblical answers to the following questions: What is death? Is death a "graduation?" Is death a friend or foe? What is the "soul?" Where are the dead? Why does God use the metaphor of "sleep" to describe death? When will the dead awaken? After laying the groundwork by answering these questions, the book deals with 13 sections of Scripture commonly used to "prove" that the "dead" are "alive." With numerous references to other Christian books and magazines, the authors show how Greek philosophy shaped the current "evangelical" doctrine of the immortality of the soul, and they briefly point out how and why the Reformation failed to reform this totally pagan belief that is now even more firmly entrenched in Christendom. COST: $5.00 (includes postage in USA; add $1 postage for overseas orders).

Dialogue

A bimonthly 16-page publication that welcomes biblical study articles, book reviews, contemporary reports or opinions on current events, personal testimonies and poems. COST: $12 per year in the USA and Canada, $18 per year overseas. (Sorry, no back issues are available).

Seminars

(All on audio cassette tape)

Introduction to God's Heart

A 24-hour Bible study series designed for any person who wants to know God and His Son Jesus Christ more intimately. The course offers the novice biblical student an overview and structure of the whole Bible, as well as the necessary keys to understanding and applying its practical truths. The more knowledgeable student will be stimulated by the in-depth details also presented. This series looks closely at such important biblical topics as (1) how we got the Bible, (2) the early chapters of Genesis versus the theory of evolution, (3) faith, (4) the new birth, (5) the Lordship of Jesus Christ, (6) speaking in tongues and more. COST: $60 (includes syllabus and postage).

Jesus Christ, The Diameter of the Ages (Parts 1-4)

This dynamic series is indispensable in understanding the most important subject of the entire Bible: Jesus Christ. It deals with His relationship with God, the Church and Israel. The series shows how Jesus saw in the Old Testament the prophecies of His birth, life, suffering, death, resurrection, ascension, exaltation and His future kingdom. Thus He was obedient to the written Word, all the way unto death on the cross. It shows what Jesus is now doing as Lord and Christ, and some things He will do when He returns to the earth to rule His kingdom. The teachings proclaim scriptural truths vital to one's knowing Jesus Christ as Lord on a daily basis, and thereby knowing God our Father. COST: $20 (includes postage).

A Journey Through the Old Testament

A 26-hour presentation designed to give you a scope and understanding of the chronology and important events of the Old Testament, which is the foundation for understanding the New Testament. As such, the teachings are full of practical keys to Christian living today. Genesis through Malachi is the same training manual that shaped the life of our Lord Jesus Christ. Much biblical geography, customs, culture and history are set forth as many biblical characters come to life in this dynamic teaching. COST: $60 (includes syllabus and postage).

Romans

An 18-hour seminar covering from beginning to end the foundational doctrinal treatise of the Church Epistles. The Book of Romans presents to the Christian the fundamental legal issue of justification by faith in Jesus Christ. It also sets forth how to win the battle between the old nature and the new nature and many practical keys to one's individual walk with the Lord. The seminar also looks at the subject of biblical Israel as compared to the Church of Grace. COST: $45 (includes postage).

Truth vs. Tradition

Designed primarily for people who already believe that the Bible is the Word of God, this 12-hour series sets in vivid contrast the logic and benefits of believing what God actually says and the illogic and consequences of believing the religious traditions of men that have infiltrated Christianity. It may be for you a stimulating refresher course that also helps you articulate you faith to others, or it may challenge you to re-evaluate your beliefs in the light of Scripture, making you more free to walk in the truth.

The Creation—Evolution Controversy

A 6-hour seminar that exposes the fallacious theory of evolution for what it really is—a religion, and not a science. The bottom line of this frontal assault on the integrity of God's Word is Satan's original lie: "You shall be as gods." The seminar defines the classical Darwinian theory of evolution and shows that it is absolutely unscientific from every angle, being totally contradicted by mathematics, genetics, thermo-dynamics, anthropology, geology, biology, zoology and the fossil record. It shows how the theory of evolution provides the rationale for such racism as evidenced by Hitler and how it has been a retardant to true scientific progress, especially in the medical field. This presentation shows what the Word of God says (and does not say) about the subject, thus giving one a clear biblical alternative to a godless lie. It includes an exposition of what is known as "the gap" between Genesis 1:1 and 1:2. COST: $20 (includes syllabus and postage).

Individual Bible Teaching Tapes

Each 90-minute audio cassette tape features a different teaching, on a variety of pertinent subjects. Yearly subscriptions are available. COST: $4 each, $24 per year; $30 overseas (includes postage). You can write CES for a list of these teachings.